RISK ASSESSMENT:

A PRACTITIONER'S GUIDE
TO PREDICTING
HARMFUL BEHAVIOUR

RISK ASSESSMENT:

A PRACTITIONER'S GUIDE
TO PREDICTING
HARMFUL BEHAVIOUR

Bryony Moore

Whiting & Birch Ltd

MCMXCVI

© Bryony Moore 1996
All rights reserved. No part of this publication may
be reproduced in any form without permission.
Whiting & Birch Ltd are registered with the
Publishers Licensing Society, London, England and
the Copyright Clearance Centre, Salem Mass. USA.
Published by Whiting & Birch Ltd,
PO Box 872, London SE23 3HL, England.
USA: Paul & Co, Publishers' Consortium Inc,
PO Box 442, Concord, MA 01742.
British Library Cataloguing in Publication Data.
A CIP catalogue record is available from
the British Library
ISBN 1 871177 84 7 (limp)
Second impression, 1998
Printed in England by Watkiss Studios

CONTENTS

To Bee Brockman, Brian Thomas-Peter
and all my colleagues at Reaside
who continue to inspire by their practice

SECTION ONE

THE CONTEXT

ONE

THE BUSINESS OF RISK

If I can't always be right, at least I can be sure

MOST PROFESSIONALS would agree that their work must be guided by certain stringent responsibilities: to the client/patient, to society, and to their agency, which includes themselves. In the blessedly straightforward case, all three are fully served by the same decision. In those which make up the bulk of the average caseload, the rights or obligations of one or more parties are compromised slightly in the interests of the others'. In the tricky or nightmare case, everyone's rights seem to be infringed, no clear benefits appear to be gained, and the professional becomes further beset by that occupational hazard, Repetitive Doubt Syndrome. The familiar symptoms of irritability, fatigue, loss of morale, premature ageing and that deep sense of being misunderstood and abused re-emerge. On a good day, we recall that this condition is, like the mystery of life, not a problem to be solved but a reality to be experienced. Too often however we respond to the syndrome by developing an artificial sense of certainty about our decisions; suspicions harden into theories, anecdotes ossify as rules and prejudices become accepted 'indicators' which guide practice and reduce anxiety.

Of course, the conscientious practitioner is rarely satisfied for long with this tenuous basis for confidence, and looks for realignment to the basic principles and beliefs which drew them into the profession in the first place. In the business of risk, regular reminders about the precarious ethical position held by decision-makers are invaluable in restoring a due sense of humility and a willingness to tolerate doubt.

THE ETHICAL DILEMMA

The many and diverse pieces of research about prediction of risk differ widely on almost every point except one; that we are not always very good at it. Some suggest that mental health professionals' predictions, for example, are no better than chance; others go so far as to maintain that we are wrong 95% of the time! While recent analyses have been more encouraging, there is still little room for complacency.

Surely, you may argue, a procedure can be justified if any potential victim can be protected by it? Even if we are only right two times out of three, surely that is better than nothing? Certainly, many of the procedures we currently rely upon can offer no better accuracy than this, and many are even less reliable. There are other factors to be taken into account, however. Consider the following illustration:

Imagine that one person in 1000 will kill.

Imagine also that an exceptionally accurate test has been devised which can predict, with 95% accuracy, those who will kill from those who will not.

In a population of 100,000, out of the 100 who would have killed, 95 will be correctly identified.

However, out of the 99,900 who will not kill, 4,995 will be identified as potential murderers.

(from Monahan 1981)

Clearly, in this case, the cost to those wrongly classified as highly risky would be enormous. The issue of whether a predictive procedure is accurate enough to justify its use, therefore, must be balanced against the cost *to those whose behaviour is being predicted* of getting it wrong.

This introduces another fundamental ethical issue, again raised by Monahan. Many of the predictions made by professionals about harmful behaviour will necessarily result in the imposition of some *restriction* on the individual concerned, and in some cases on those closest to them. This may involve reduced access to their children, constraints on where they may live, refusal of parole, an increase in the level of supervision which they must tolerate or compulsory admission to psychiatric hospital. Furthermore, this restriction is imposed not precisely because of what they have done (as is a punitive fine, for example, in the case of a theft); it is because of *what they have not yet done*. Thomas Szasz, the renowned 'anti-psychiatry' crusader of the 1970s has commented that this constitutes a '... basic violation of most fundamental of human rights ... punishment for past wrongs, not future ones'.

Further ethical, as well as practical, issues involve:

- the timing of the assessment, and the use made of its conclusions,
- the choice of the individual/s who will carry it out.

Timing and purpose

Many calculations of risk are inevitably made at a crisis point in the management of a case and therefore in the life of the client, who has everything to lose and so is strongly motivated to present themselves as non-harmful. They are frequently disbelieved as a result (we tend to weigh heavily a person's potential gain when evaluating their truthfulness) and mutual suspiciousness severely damages the chance of working together in the future. Assessments designed, on the other hand, to encourage longer term *risk management* rather than a simple yes/no decision are therefore likely to increase accuracy of prediction as well as reducing the hostility of all concerned.

Who should undertake the assessment?

Thought should be given to the choice of professional making the risk assessment, both by the individual concerned and their managers. The worker already most closely involved in the case is usually chosen, either because of limited agency resources, the worker's familiarity with the client and his/her history, or a more diffuse sense of 'case-worker loyalty' by all concerned.

In many cases, this may be quite inappropriate, for a number of reasons. For example:

- All other factors being equal, greater familiarity with an individual is known to lead to a *reduced* perception of their riskiness. We have all known those long-term clients with files the thickness of the London phone directory, who with their families seem to veer from crisis to crisis, who have been on the caseload of almost every member of the department and who seem almost as much a part of the place as those on the payroll. While those who know them best may well be in the strongest position to make accurate predictions about them, the same workers are also likely to be the most complacent, and influenced by a belief that the agency can contain any problems likely to arise, rather than on an objective evaluation of risk factors, probability and cost.

- Another example of inappropriate 'insider' assessment would be one in which the key worker or their team have developed such strong emotional investment in the outcome of the evaluation that they are no longer able to suspend this in the interests of accurate decision-making. They may not be motivated, for instance, to search out facts which would weaken their argument, or may accept inadequate evidence as support of their own views.

In both these situations, an outsider is often better placed to carry out the assessment. Sometimes, a specialist service will be called for, while other teams may have reciprocal arrangements with other disciplines or with colleagues in a neighbouring team to provide this objectivity.

A contrasting type of case typically involves a vulnerable, highly defended client who has built up a trusting relationship with their key worker; the worker, however, feels that s/he lacks the specialist skills to assess risk in the case, and makes a referral to another professional. The client is unable to relate to the newcomer, may perceive that their case has been labelled as more serious, feels anxious and suspicious, and may even lose faith in their key worker for exposing them to this intrusion. In such cases, it should be possible for the keyworker to call in the *consultative* services of the outside specialist, who will provide a structured framework for the risk assessment as well as any independent professional angle relevant to the case. While this may produce a less 'pure', independent assessment, it will immeasurably strengthen the only one possible. Such flexibility and integration of different approaches are fundamental to reliable assessment of risk.

CHARACTERISTICS OF A SOUND RISK ASSESSMENT FRAMEWORK

Most practitioners look to an assessment procedure to increase the accuracy of their predictions, make the most of their skills and reduce their anxieties. In risk assessment, the procedure adopted will need to prompt the following processes.

1. *Defining the behaviour to be predicted.*
   It is, firstly, important to focus assessment on the potentially harmful behaviour rather than the 'dangerous' individual.
   It is also essential to assess each worrying behaviour individually, as each is likely to involve different risk factors. Grouping anticipated types of conduct together can significantly reduce accuracy of prediction.

2. *Distinguishing between probability and cost of the behaviour*
   When an event is said to be low-risk, do you mean that it's unlikely to happen, that it wouldn't matter much if it did happen, or that there's not enough information to conclude much either way?
   Unless the assessment distinguishes between the *seriousness* of the anticipated conduct and the *likelihood* of its occurrence, it is unlikely to be able to weigh the facts appropriately or provide any reliable basis for decision-making.

3. *Awareness of probable sources of error*
   The degree of confidence in our predictions can vary enormously from one assessment to another. This tends to be the result either of the type and quality of the information available, or of the amount of error. Error can arise from attributes of:

   i)   the person being assessed (for example, their unattractive manner or their poor reliability as an informant),
   ii) the assessor (a difficulty in suspending personal values, for instance), *and*
   iii) the context (such as an agency bias in favour of one or other party involved).

   It is unrealistic to expect any assessment to be error-free, but awareness, constant monitoring and adjustment are essential throughout.

4. *Taking into account both internal and external factors*
   Almost all behaviour is the result of interaction between characteristics of the individual (for example attitudes,

needs, skills, controls) and those of the environment (demands, constraints, stressors etc). An understanding of these two sources of influence on the target behaviour, as well as the balance between them, is crucial to any prediction.

5. *Checking whether all necessary information has been gathered*
   In some assessments, few sources of data may be needed in the development of a strong formulation; that is, an understanding of the mechanism of the behaviour. However, when the assessor feels dissatisfied with the accuracy of their work, a checklist can be invaluable in helping to establish whether this low level of confidence is due to missing or low-quality information.

   Many professionals are required to make evaluations of future harm on the basis of entirely inadequate or irrelevant material, and it is important in such cases to be able to qualify any predictions made and state what their limitations are. The assessor is then in a position to educate managers and policy-makers in the kind of data necessary to increase predictive accuracy.

6. *Identifying if / when specialists or other outsiders need to be involved*
   One of the most common weaknesses identified in risk assessment is the tendency for it to be carried out by single disciplines, or even individuals. The range of information necessary is rarely to be found within the training and expertise of one profession, and predictive accuracy is likely to be compromised as a result.

   In such cases, it is the front-line practitioners who are likely to be held responsible when predictions about risk fall short. They therefore have the most to gain by maintaining the pressure to improve inter-agency cooperation. In each assessment where the need for outside/specialist input is identified, the assessor should declare this clearly and state how their own predictions have been compromised by this lack of input. A thorough assessment procedure will prompt such identification.

7. *Planning key interventions*
   Because a sound assessment of risk will be based on the formulation of the mechanisms underlying the behaviour, it will automatically identify those processes which appear to be key elements in increasing or reducing such risk. These

may involve only the assessed individual (for example, where a crucial skills deficit or deviant drive is highlighted), or may extend to others (where marital stressors or difficulty in relating to residential staff may be identified triggers, for instance). In cases where the resources needed to address the identified issue are not available, the professional should nevertheless state the requirement in their recommendations, so that a realistic picture of clients' needs continues to be generated.

8. *Prediction of factors likely to increase / decrease future risk*
    A risk assessment should not be viewed as a one-off snapshot of the current potential for harm, but rather a continuing process, to be frequently modified and updated. If the formulation is comprehensive and sound, it should be possible to anticipate some of the events likely to occur in the future and how these would affect the risk posed. Some of these events may constitute warning signs that action is necessary by one or more of the supervising professionals; good practice would indicate that these should be identified to all concerned in advance (including, as far as possible, the individual being assessed) in advance, and the reactions planned and agreed. Too often, entirely foreseeable developments trigger inconsistent, knee-jerk responses from workers who have an insufficient framework of understanding against which to measure events, and who therefore have to respond largely to their own anxieties, or those of their own supervisors.

CONCLUSION

Hallmarks of a robust risk assessment procedure, therefore, include:

1. Guidelines for developing a valid formulation of the target behaviour, which is refined and modified over time.
2. Strategies for monitoring and addressing ethical issues and sources of error .
3. Clear indicators for action, for all concerned.
4. Full and efficient communication between practitioner and manager, such that the needs of the assessor and assessed continue to influence policy and resource allocation.

TWO

SOURCES OF ERROR

ERROR TYPES

WHEN A judgement is to be made about risk, there are four possible outcomes.

Imagine that a prediction has to be made about whether something harmful will or will not occur. (In the majority of risk assessments, of course, the issue is one of *degrees* of risk, but for the sake of simplicity, it is assumed here that a yes/no prediction is required.)

In the table below, the predicted risk is compared to the actual outcome.

		PREDICTION	
		YES	NO
OUTCOME	YES	A TRUE POSITIVE PREDICTION	B FALSE NEGATIVE PREDICTION (TYPE II ERROR)
	NO	C FALSE POSITIVE PREDICTION (TYPE I ERROR)	D TRUE NEGATIVE PREDICTION

As the table shows, the prediction of the harmful event could be right in one of two ways:

Box A It was predicted, and it happened
Box D It was not predicted, and did not happen.

It could also be wrong in two ways:

Box B It was not predicted, but it happened
Box C It was predicted, but it did not happen.

The terms 'Type I Error' and 'Type II Error' are used in research statistics to describe the situations where either a relationship between variables is falsely predicted, or turns out to exist even though not predicted. A wealth of strategies exist in research methodology to reduce the chances of one or other type of error occurring, although always at the expense of the other being increased.

ERROR AND ETHICS

While the issue of under- and over-prediction may pose an interesting, even infuriating, problem for the researcher; for the professional caseworker it can represent a far more grievous dilemma; sometimes quite literally one of life and death. The two types of error carry hugely different consequences for both the person doing the predicting and the person whose behaviour they predict.

Consider a case where it is predicted that a parent previously violent to a child is unacceptably likely to inflict further injury in the course of unsupervised access. If the prediction is false, and no harm would have occurred (*false positive error*), the cost is to the person assessed as risky, and to their family, but *who is to know?* From the position of the agency concerned, it is a potential injury successfully prevented. If, on the other hand, the access is considered safe, and harm occurs (*false negative error*), the consequences to all concerned can be enormous. The child is hurt, the family complains of inadequate protection, the offending parent may have lost their last chance of family life, the worker suffers emotionally and perhaps professionally and the agency risks that most dreaded of fates, another tabloid headline shrieking incompetence and demanding vengeance. Little wonder, then, that many professionals err on the side of caution, whenever they can get away with it. Calculated false positives are often considered unofficially acceptable, in practice.

Another factor, however, operates in some cases as a counterbalance to blanket over-prediction of risk. While arenas such as the mental health and child protection fields are *intolerant of false negative estimates* ('Social workers fail to protect battered child'; 'Rapist escapes while on home leave from clinic'), the criminal justice system is designed to *discourage unsubstantiated false positive predictions*. The principle that it is better for nine guilty people to go free than for one innocent one to be punished ensures that any positive risk assessment put before a court has to bear up to considerable scrutiny. Anyone who has been required to defend their damning report against a skilled barrister will be all too aware that their argument has to be well substantiated and presented if it is to survive the ordeal. Worrying rumours or bizarre, but possibly irrelevant, events in the case which understandably cause the practitioner so much anxiety are frequently too vague to be admissible as evidence.

Those professionals, then, who operate in the overlap between the criminal justice system and the mental health or child protection fields are especially caught on the horns of this dilemma.

While undeniably uncomfortable, however, it is a situation destined to improve practice. One only needs to observe an agency or team who are allowed to operate entirely by their own rules and theories, whose methods are mysterious to outsiders and whose decisions cannot be challenged, to recognise that controls are needed, and not only for the sake of those wrongly condemned by such a system. If fashion dictates for a time that a particular group may be freely discriminated against (a carte blanche to over-predict riskiness), the inevitable backlash is liable to create a situation where gross under-prediction is imposed. This reversal in attitudes already occurs outside the realm of risk assessment in relation to previously underprotected groups. Misguided professional 'political correctness', for example, may now result in a complainant who is female, from an ethnic minority, or gay or lesbian benefiting from biased decision-making which is officially sanctioned (especially if the accused falls into none of these categories), whereas in the past they were likely to suffer from distorted unofficial prejudice.

It is worth thinking, then, about the groups who are currently considered undeserving of objective treatment. How might an attitudinal or legal backlash affect decision-making about those groups in the future? Suspected male sexual offenders against children, for example, are often the victims of some of the worst professional decision-making, and theirs is far too dangerous a behaviour to be handled so clumsily. We cannot afford, morally or pragmatically, to view any group as fair game for wholesale over-positive prediction on the basis that no-one will ever know (or care) if we were wrong.

At a symposium on The Assessment and Treatment of Sex Offenders in New Zealand several years ago, the list of contributors was circulated the night before, and included to my great surprise a spokesman from the national Sex Offenders' Support Association. An ex-offender, no less! Having been confident until that point that my paper was fair and well-phrased, I nevertheless spent much of the rest of the evening double-checking my notes for any pejorative terms, unsupported 'facts' or confident references to weak studies. It came as an unpleasant shock to realise that I was probably in a similar situation to an evangelical speaker against alcoholism in the 1950s who encounters for the first time on the conference platform an articulate, informed ex-drinker who is there professionally to represent fellow AA members. The shock on this occasion was caused not so much by his presence - after all, who better to be involved in the event? - but by my own reaction to it. I had come to accept that those who were fundamental to the 'problem' were irrelevant as participants in, and critics of, the solution. In the event, it transpired that the speaker in question was actually a volunteer counsellor rather than an ex-offender himself. The experience, however, remained a singularly humbling one for me and reinforced my belief that professionals making assessments about potentially risky individuals need to examine the soundness of their decision-making rigorously and continuously. This duty must be even more scrupulously observed where the individual concerned has little real power to challenge the process or its outcome.

ERROR ARISING FROM INADEQUATE KNOWLEDGE

Most professionals would accept that 'the best predictor of future behaviour is past behaviour', yet many risk assessments are carried out using only a fraction of the historical data potentially available. The difficulties caused may fall into the following categories.

Lack of information about the person to be assessed

Many practitioners are acutely aware of their lack of necessary facts in arriving at an assessment of risk. The gaps may be genuinely due to time or resource constraints externally imposed, or to obstacles placed in the way of obtaining material from other agencies. Frequently, however, it is simply outside customary practice to seek such additional information.

In order to establish diverse data collection as routine, it can be useful to ask the client/patient to sign a consent form early in the assessment process. Quite apart from the ethical desirability of such a step, its very presence in the file tends to act as a prompt throughout the work. The business of discussing where useful information may be sought can also give a useful breadth to the interviews, and can serve to reassure the client that opinions favourable to them will be sought as well as negative ones.

Clearly an advantage of this wider view is that new information may come to light which allows shifts in the worker's understanding of the individual and their behaviour. Where the previously available facts may emphasise a person's unusual reactions, for example, details of even more unusual demands made by their situation, or a lack of opportunities for learning appropriate responses may be revealed. An individual who presents as socially fluent and 'streetwise' may have been discovered in the past to have marked learning difficulties. Someone thought to be a first time violent offender may be discovered to have committed similar acts of violence for which they were never convicted, being dealt with instead by the psychiatric services.

New information may also give new meaning *to loosely connected facts*

Additional data from other departments or agencies may also reveal important information about the *generalisability* of the behaviour in question. Someone who is known to have been dangerously impulsive in one situation may be discovered to have quite adequate controls in other, very similar ones. Violent episodes towards staff in an institution might be found to constitute the only examples of aggression in an individual's history, and could reveal a link with specific anxiety, victim behaviour or temporary mental disturbance.

Of course, past information from other disciplines may not be limited to clear-cut facts whose meaning is evident. In cases where *summaries, inferences and interpretations* must be made

Case Example

A middle-aged man accused of sexual abuse of his step-daughter had no previous convictions for child abuse. However, in his youth he had been found guilty of numerous sexual offences with cows and horses. Professionals were perturbed as to whether this past predilection was an indication of greater risk to his children or not. It could mean that he indiscriminately targeted vulnerable victims in an opportunistic way, or it could reflect a quite unconnected penchant for livestock. His criminal record was no help, recording only property offences. However, the police microfiche records, which provide a descriptive paragraph about past offences, were obtained; they revealed that one of his burglaries had involved the attempted rape of the elderly householder, who as a result of the assault was too disturbed to give evidence against him. It was then possible to make a satisfactory case for the 'vulnerable victim' formulation. His partner was also motivated to take a more serious view of her children's need for protection as a result of this information coming to light.

about others' work, it is rarely appropriate for this to be done by anyone except the original author. If this is not possible, someone from their profession should be consulted, in order to ensure that the intended meaning is retained. The author will also be able to advise on the *validity* of applying their old conclusions to the current situation.

Check too that the *confidentiality* constraints applying to the information are not violated by its inclusion in your report. Anyone who has suffered the experience of having their views distorted into an unrecognisable 'summary' by someone else, whose assessment is misapplied to a quite different situation, or who has been quoted in another report which is then circulated to people who were never intended to be privy to the original, will appreciate the importance of these professional courtesies.

Accounts gathered from *individuals who have known the client and/or victim for some time* are often invaluable in corroborating or contradicting their views of events. Some agencies such as Social Services, Probation and the Police tend to collect such accounts as a matter of course; mental health workers, including psychologists, seem to be among the worst culprits in ignoring these invaluable independent sources of information. As well as providing a crucial insight into the historical context of the behaviour, these significant others can also act as *monitors* of change once intervention has begun.

The assessed individual should also be encouraged to provide as much information as possible about their target behaviour. This may seem too obvious to need mentioning, but in reality it is too often assumed that the client will be so motivated to appear acceptable that their accounts will be useless. A number of studies have shown that self-report, for example of violent assaults, significantly improves predictive accuracy. This is likely to be the case particularly in a continuing, rather than snapshot, assessment.

Finally, a word on the *availability* of past information. The lamentable practice, often statutorily imposed on institutions and agencies, of destroying professional records after a few years has made the task of informed risk assessment unnecessarily difficult. Special Schools and Child Guidance Teams, whose accumulated observations, assessments and opinions regarding the early life of a troubled and troublesome child would provide vital insights into later deviancy, are required to shred their files after a minimal period. Disregarding the evidence that some offending behaviours tend to re-emerge cyclically throughout the life cycle, Probation departments have to dispose of all but a skeleton of their old notes and reports. Frequently, crucial facts are gained only by virtue of the inefficiency of individual teams in adhering to the shredding policy or the capacity of their storage shelves.

It should go without saying that restrictions on the access to such material have to be established and applied rigorously if civil rights are to be protected. However, there is an equally powerful argument in favour of ensuring the protection of the information, if later developments in the individual's life are to be understood fully and informed decisions made.

Assessment by a single discipline

Until now we have been concerned with means of strengthening the individual practitioner's assessment by adding past findings of others to the picture. By far the most thorough approach to assessing present and future risk, however, is by multiprofessional teamwork.

One of the most significant factors known to limit predictive accuracy is assessment by a single discipline. This can lead to

---

Case Example

A team considering episodes of domestic violence by a young man felt fairly confident, towards the end of the assessment, that their working hypothesis was proving sufficient to account for the assaults. Their formulation identified violent role models in childhood, leading to a learned aggressive behaviour against a background of limited empathy, high anxiety levels and inability to manage conflict assertively. When the Senior Registrar on the team carried out her interview, however, she recognised elements in the violent episodes which could be characteristic of temporal lobe epilepsy. Subsequent EEG testing confirmed this, and anti-epileptic medication reduced the frequency of violent episodes to a fraction of their previous level. Following re-assessment, cognitive-behavioural work successfully addressed the remaining difficulties.

---

error in various ways, including the narrow range of measures used, lack of training in interpretation of certain data, restricted access to other documentation, and an inability to recognise the signs that factors outside their expertise may be involved.

While routine screening by several disciplines is ideal, many cases may be identified at the outset as apparently falling within the competence of one or two professionals, who tend to become key case workers or coordinators of the assessment. Good practice should then encourage frequent opportunities for multidisciplinary discussion of the case, in order to allow the other team members a consultative role.

A word about the responsibilities of this sort of team working

When multidisciplinary Mental Health Resource Teams were first established in the community, many were tempted to operate as though they were composed of generic workers or 'therapists', with little acknowledgement of the different training and skills basic to each discipline. (On more than one occasion, when phoning a local MHRT, I have had the indelicacy to ask the profession of the person answering the phone, and received a response which rather suggested that they had been asked what colour underwear they were wearing!) Claiming unique expertise seemed almost to be regarded as unacceptable elitism. There are, however, very clear legal obligations on every professional to ensure the allocation of tasks appropriately within their team *according to the core skills of the disciplines represented.* It is therefore essential that the team agrees at the outset on how these skills are distributed among them, which are shared, and which are missing altogether.

Finally, singlehanded assessments commonly occur because of the real or imagined isolation of the assessor from others. Many professionals have little knowledge of the availability of help from within their agency or elsewhere; others identify such support, only to be told that it is outside the departmental budget or otherwise inappropriate. In such cases, it is the front-line practitioner who is likely to be held responsible when predictions about risk fall short. They therefore have the most to gain by maintaining the pressure to improve inter-agency cooperation. *In each assessment where the need for outside / specialist input is indicated, the final report should identify this clearly and state how the assessor's own predictions have been weakened or restricted by the lack of such input.*

IGNORANCE OF THE RELEVANT BASE-RATES

The base rate is the known frequency of a phenomenon occurring in a given population; the figure that tells you the likelihood of the predicted behaviour *in cases of this sort.* This is the area of risk assessment known as *actuarial prediction.*

Frequently, before you even begin to consider factors of the individual case, you will need to look at the actuarial indicators— *the likelihood of a person like this behaving in this way.*

Ignorance of the relevant base rate for a behaviour is probably the single most common source of error, and can give an extremely misleading picture. Imagine, for example, the effect of a news item stating that escapes from your county's prisons had doubled over the last ten years, if it did not also state that in the current decade there had been just two escapes, and in the decade before that, only one. Sometimes distortion can arise from quoting the statistics from an unhelpful angle. A recent and much-quoted statement on urban crime, for instance, suggested that the majority of muggings in London were perpetrated by young Afro-Caribbean men. Whether or not this is true, a more helpful statistic would be the proportion of young Afro-Caribbean men who offend in this way; a minority of that sub-population.

Case Example

In a recent risk assessment presented as expert evidence in court, I was asked to estimate the probability of harm being caused to a child by her severely depressed mother. My previous report to a case conference had indicated significant risk that she could kill the child and then herself while depressed. The court was told that the mother was in the group identified as most at risk of that behaviour in the UK. Of the 7 identified high risk signs for murder-suicide, the mother had at least 6. (I was not qualified to give a view on the 7th, which was a biochemical factor.) How likely does that make the behaviour? Practically inevitable? 85% likely? In fact the probability was way below 50%; even individuals qualifying for all 7 high risk factors are far more likely not to commit the act than they are to commit it.

The court needed to be informed of the actual base rate for the behaviour in this small and vulnerable population (ie depressed mothers), just as they needed to know about the presence of the risk indicators themselves.

Some behaviours are misattributed with mythical base rates. Middle-aged male sex offenders who abuse children, for example, are generally accepted to be notorious recidivists. This means that anyone required to assess the risk of reoffending in such an individual could expect to start with a view of *high probability risk and work downwards*. In fact, research indicates that the majority of these offenders are not reconvicted of similar crimes after their first conviction. The minority who are reconvicted, often many times, are thought to account for a disproportionate share of the total number of victims between them. It might therefore be more appropriate for the assessor to *begin with a prediction of low probability and work upwards from that* on the basis of individual factors. Similarly, research during the 1970s which looked at clinical predictions of violence among discharged psychiatric patients found that the most accurate prediction in all studies was a negative one; the prediction that no violence would occur. Other types of offences, such as the stealing of cars by teenagers, are known to have high recidivism rates: this knowledge is an important starting point for any assessment, as well as for the intervention which follows.

> **Case Example**
>
> A sex offender was referred for a psychosexual risk assessment, having previously been identified as 'high risk' following interviews with an individual mental health worker. It transpired that the main assessment technique employed had involved asking the offender to name his favourite nursery rhyme and drawing conclusions from his choice. The unfortunate client, after some understandable resistance (which was noted with disapproval), admitted that he liked 'Hansel and Gretel'. Big mistake! The themes of abduction, illegal imprisonment and child cannibalism were claimed to highlight previously unsuspected areas of deviant interest. Because of its spurious theoretical basis, the interpretations derived from this 'assessment' were quashed. The full psychosexual screening by the team later concluded similarly that the client presented a high level of risk, but did so using established procedures supported by theory and research, which bore rigorous scrutiny in the subsequent court hearing.
>
> (Later, an impromptu poll among the team members revealed that Hansel and Gretel was also a popular choice with them, largely due to the appeal of the gingerbread house.)

USE OF INVALID MODELS OR INSTRUMENTS

Few professionals have the time or the material to keep fully abreast of the latest developments in every aspect of their work. Many focus on keeping informed about one or two key areas, others make piecemeal advances when the opportunity arises, a few carry on using increasingly hazy memories of the state of the art at the time of their training. Thus most of us probably persevere with pet theories and favourite techniques with which we feel comfortable and which by and large support our intuition, despite the fact that they may no longer be the most accurate or efficient way of doing the job.

Fortunately, idiosyncratic practices may actually be well founded. One of the most rewarding aspects of attending a conference or training event, after all, is discovering that recent research has at last confirmed one's long-established approach! In new fields, too, experimental approaches have often to be used until empirically demonstrated sound or otherwise. Generally, though, it is considered professionally negligent to impose unproven or outmoded methods on clients/patients where more valid, reliable or ethically sound alternatives exist.

SOURCES OF ERROR

No one is completely free from bias, the tendency to distort perception according to one's own needs and values. Few perhaps would choose to be, given that bias is probably proportionate to the emotional commitment felt for particular aims, ideals, theories and client groups; the very commitment in fact which drew most people to their 'caring profession' initially. While most scrupulous practitioners attempt to cultivate self-awareness and counter-balances to their own particular biases, it can also be useful to consider the general sources of bias which affect everyone.

ATTRIBUTIONAL BIAS

No matter how much information about the individual one adds to the predictive equation, one cannot bring about the correlation co-efficient between individual characteristics and prediction criteria much above 0.40 (Monahan 1981).

In other words, if you knew everything there was to know about an individual in isolation, it would only enable you to be right in your predictions about them 40% of the time. In order to improve on this level of accuracy, you would have to gain some understanding of how the person responds to external factors.

There are a number of fundamental differences between the ways we perceive others' actions and our own. A major difference concerns the perceived source of influences on behaviour. In general, the more closely we identify with the person whose behaviour is being explained, *the more likely we are to overemphasise the external causes*. When the other person is seen as very different (for example, is a psychiatric patient, an offender, or from an unfamiliar culture), *we are most likely to over-attribute their conduct to internal drives*. Rather than seeing it as situation-specific and amenable to influence (like our own behaviour), we will probably see it as fairly central to their character or condition, and unlikely to change.

This phenomenon of over-internalising pervades our judgement at all levels, from views on our partner's driving, to suspicions that a victim has 'asked for it', or to assumptions that the mentally ill person has been assaultative purely because of his psychosis. In the case of professional judgement, the reverse effect often develops as the client concerned becomes more familiar to the worker. Residential staff, or those who carry out intensive therapeutic

21

> **Example**
>
> Take angry outbursts in team meetings. Occasionally I lose my temper because I am, frankly, surrounded by idiots. I am an intelligent person, with high professional standards and important insights, who is trying to achieve the best possible outcome: when I repeatedly meet unnecessary obstacles, negligence and stupidity, I become angry. And when my colleague loses her temper? It is clear to me that she is a bad-tempered type with poor controls, who is sadly over-involved; she is driven by her own personality difficulties, distorted views and the need to get her own way. In other words, I see myself as a reasonable person whose anger is triggered by external events, while I perceive her anger as largely a result of internal factors.

work, naturally begin to understand the behaviour from the client's viewpoint, and learn more about the environmental triggers which influenced it. Conflicts can then arise between them and others whose focus is the damage done, and who in turn are sharply aware of the individual's deviance or weakness.

Here is another strength of teamworking, because the truth usually lies somewhere between the two positions, and the most effective management of the risk will be based on accurate balancing of both sets of factors, internal and external.

SOURCES OF ERROR

When two events or phenomena are shown to be related, they are often said to be correlated.

Example

If Factor A (eg suicide rate) increases and decreases when Factor B (eg unemployment) similarly goes up and down, they are said to be *positively correlated.*

If the probability of Factor X (eg voting Conservative) is greater when Factor Y (eg intelligence) is lower, then intelligence and voting Conservative are said to be *negatively correlated.*

Where the change in one factor does not appear to be associated with any variation in the other (eg star sign and shoe size), there is said to be *no correlation.*

One of the most common errors in judgement is to assume that *correlation implies causality*; that because two things are strongly related, that one causes the other. Have another look at the first example in the box above. Did you make the assumption that unemployment *causes* an increase in the suicide rate ? Or, in the second example, that stupidity *leads to* a Tory vote? Both may be true, of course, but not necessarily. It may be the case, for instance, that *poverty* is the crucial link between unemployment and suicide; that those with a low income are more likely to attempt suicide regardless of whether they are in work or not, and that for the well-off, unemployment does not increase their suicide risk. The unemployment/suicide correlation would be strengthened by the fact that for the majority, unemployment and poverty are likely to occur together.

As you may have noticed from these examples, it is easier to assume a causal relationship falsely when the correlation is somehow consistent with one's own beliefs.

If a study indicated a high correlation between convictions for vandalism and having a skinhead haircut, for instance, this could lead to a number of immediate causal interpretations, according to one's prior viewpoint. These may include:

1. Vandals tend to like looking, as well as acting, aggressively.
2. Taking on the appearance of an antisocial subculture encourages deviant behaviour.
3. Youths who look conspicuously anti-establishment are more

likely to be arrested and convicted, regardless of guilt.
4. Excessive cold to the head causes a pituitary imbalance, increasing disinhibited behaviour. (This of course is entirely fictional, but thinking about it, how many woolly bobble-hatted vandals have you seen?)

Some interesting research, looking at the way clinicians and others arrive at their judgements, indicates how many conclusions can be based on false correlations. The practitioner's existing beliefs can prove more powerful in influencing their perception than do new facts about the case. 'Such pseudo-scientific descriptions have been reiterated so often that they have become part of the accepted mythology of clinical practice' (Diamond 1974). Even the less formalised 'correlations', those which may be unconscious, or which one would hesitate to pass on to a student, can be extremely significant in decision-making.

Example

An 'audit' of the correlations regularly used by a team in their evaluations of clients can be an invigorating exercise. In my own workshops, pairs of course members are provided with different offence types, or other sub-groups within the client population, and given 20 minutes to generate as many factors which may be associated with high and low risk as they can think of (even the most tenuous or ethically unsound). The results are often highly amusing, but also stimulate invaluable discussion. Factors 'linked' with risk of future violence, for instance, have included tattoos on the knuckles, rude slogans on T-shirts, lateness for appointments and addressing a female probation officer as `Darling'!

Among those characteristics often thought to contribute to a lower assessment of risk have been physical attractiveness, intelligence, a good sense of humour and regular claims that the professional is helping the client a lot. What all these 'correlations' have in common is a lack of theoretical basis and no empirical support. Who could be certain, however, that their own judgement is never influenced by equally unsubstantiated factors ?

Selectivity bias involves a distortion at the information collection stage. It highlights our tendency to tap only those sources which will support rather than falsify predictions, particularly positive ones. In collecting the information necessary to make a sound risk assessment, therefore, try to give particular attention to sources and material which could provide contradictory evidence. This may feel at times like a foolish exercise in making life more difficult for yourself, but it can pay dividends.

Case Example

A middle-aged man who had served a 5 year prison sentence for rape was arrested on suspicion of a similar offence. At first he protested that he had been living in another town 200 miles to the north at the time of the incident, but without undue pressure soon went on to confess and provided incriminating detail about the offence that seemed certain to convict him. He repeated this confession to his solicitor, adding that he was constantly fantasising about rape and had carried it out on numerous other occasions. The lawyer, however, who was new to this client, made more thorough investigations and interviewed the suspect's family, who confirmed his first account. His landlady in the northern town further supported his alibi for the night in question. It further transpired that while the man, a fanatical football fan, had been working away from home, his father had sent him the local Saturday sports paper, so that he could keep up with the news of his favourite team. The details of the offence which had formed such a crucial part of his confession had been printed in that week's edition of the paper, and the suspect was later found to have cut out and kept the article, adding to his extensive collection of literature on violent sexual assault. The case against the man soon disintegrated.

The solicitor's curiosity then encouraged him to go back to the details of the earlier conviction, where a similar pattern of denial then full confession began to emerge. He took more seriously records of his client's original half-hearted claim that he had been 'locked up' at the time the first rape had occurred; investigations at the local police station confirmed that he had indeed been held in the cells for questioning over some minor property offence for the whole of that night.

The man had a preoccupation with rape as well as a

compulsion to be seen as a dangerous sexual predator, and had served a five year sentence for a crime to which he had confessed. Who, given his history and presentation, would have doubted that he was guilty of the second offence and bothered to check the facts?

CONFIRMATION BIAS

There is another important way in which we distort decision-making systematically, and which is often misinterpreted as purely motivational (driven by our own best interests), and even deliberate. It concerns *the weight we give to particular elements of the available information.* In a situation such as a court hearing, where all parties might have an identical sheaf of papers, the emphasis given by each of them to individual items of evidence is likely to vary widely.

When people are asked to test out tentative predictions which they have developed, they are likely to pick test examples which will support their hypotheses rather than contradict them. This can be a fairly conscious strategy, as we all know; when brooding over the selfishness of one's family, one tends to conjure up enough past sins of this type to prove the point beyond all doubt (until the family is criticised by an unwelcome outsider, of course, when plenty of evidence of their considerate behaviour suddenly becomes available!) When a professional is known to have taken a strong position for or against a particular outcome in a case, they will often feel motivated to 'prove themselves right' by emphasising only those facts which strengthen their argument and weaken others'. They act, in fact, more like lawyers whose task is to win a case, rather than like judges who seek to establish the truth. When one individual adopts this biased position, it also tends to reduce the ability of those who disagree to maintain objectivity.

Research on human problem-solving, however, has shown that at least part of this process is pre-conscious. One experiment, using a simple logic puzzle, demonstrated that even when subjects had no emotional investment in one solution being correct rather than another one, they persisted in looking only for evidence to support, rather than weaken, the one they had thought of. It was concluded that 'subjects confirm, not because they want to, but because they cannot think of the way to falsify'.

(In another important published work on bias, an analysis of the Cleveland Enquiry illustrates how this resistance, whether cognitive or motivational, can contribute to error on a massive and catastrophic scale.)

> A fundamental lapse in logic to which confirmation bias can lead is:
>
> ### If A = B, then B = A
>
> eg All mothers are women
> Therefore all women are mothers. *or*
>
> Sexual abuse is known to cause certain emotional problems
> Therefore the presence of those problems means that sexual abuse has occurred

Clearly, it is essential that a professional considering the importance of the various factors which make up their risk assessment stops to challenge their hypotheses at regular intervals. One may ask, for instance:

- 'What hard evidence do I have to support my hypothesis/prediction?'
- 'Are there other possible explanations for what I have observed?'
- 'How would I demonstrate that one of those other explanations is the correct one, if I wanted to?'

If the argument for one interpretation seems to you overwhelmingly strong, asking an uninvolved colleague to play Devil's Advocate can be a revealing exercise. Alternatively, imagine that a close member of your family has become the client/victim of an incompetent team, and that the same argument is being levelled at them. How would you start to challenge it?

WHY WE MAY NOT BE AS BAD AT IT AS WE LOOK

As already established, research on the frequency of accurate prediction of harm does not look impressive. Monahan commented in 1981 that 'Psychiatrists and Psychologists are accurate in no more than one out of three predictions of violent behaviour over a several-year period among institutionalised populations that had both committed violence in the past (and thus had high base rates for it) and who were diagnosed as mentally ill'. Among less clearly defined groups, even lower success rates would be anticipated.

However, it is important to take into account two complicating factors, both affecting positive prediction (that is, the view that harm is likely). Although over-prediction of harm certainly occurs, for reasons already discussed, it probably happens less often than would appear at first glance.

Let us say that members of a particular group are predicted to have a 60% chance of re-offending in two years, and at the end of that period only 25% appear to have done so. How likely is it that one of the following factors has affected the outcome ?

Under-reporting

Recidivism figures tend to be obtained from official sources, often re-arrest or re-conviction rates. For many reasons, these are likely to understate the true offending figures, particularly among those with mental disorder and prior contact with the psychiatric services, who may well be diverted from the criminal-justice system before formal charges have been brought.

As already mentioned, the figures may also under-represent the true reoffending rate because the offenders themselves are not asked to contribute information. Again, the actions may go unreported by victims, because of fear or through sympathy with the offender's difficulties. This is more likely in certain crimes, such as offending within the home, where the negative consequences of reporting are often perceived as greater than the consequences of keeping quiet..

Prevention

Finally, risk assessment is designed ultimately to reduce future harm, and those thought most likely to cause harm will usually be subject to the most rigorous preventative strategies. Prisoners assessed as high risk may be refused parole; those discharged psychiatric patients believed to be more vulnerable are likely to receive closer follow-up, and their symptoms of relapse responded to more urgently. Abusing parents may be refused access to their children; those known to have made the most serious suicide attempts could be offered more intensive psychological therapy.

In other words, when we have predicted that there is a risk of dangerous behaviour, we tend to make strenuous attempts to avert it. *The paradox lies in the fact that successful prediction should actually lead to prevention, and thus prove itself wrong.*

SECTION TWO

FACTORS IN INDIVIDUAL RISK

Assessment of the risk presented by an individual is a process involving the following questions:

- What is the behaviour to be predicted?
- What is the probability of the behaviour occurring?
- What is the likely cost of the behaviour?

In this section we consider the reasons for asking these questions, the types of information which may need to be gathered in order to answer them and the factors to be considered when weighting their relative importance, or predictive validity.

Together, these chapters emphasise *the importance of building a formulation* of the behaviour in question.

A formulation is a proposed model of the process which has led to the behaviour. It attempts to clarify the predisposing influences, choice of victim, disinhibitors, drives, triggers, functions, and rewards. It will allow the assessor to suggest answers to the fundamental questions: *Why this act? Why in this way? Why now?*

THREE

DEFINITION OF THE TARGET BEHAVIOUR

IT MAY seem too obvious to need stating that, in order to predict the likelihood of an act, it is necessary first to define it. However, it is a common error to miss out this vital stage because it is assumed that everyone knows what they are looking for; it usually ensures that the process is off on the wrong foot before anyone is aware that it has actually started.

So what purpose does definition serve?

'Dangerousness' is not a useful concept in risk assessment.

For one thing, it implies a pervasive quality, characteristic of a person in much the same way that talkativeness or generosity may be thought characteristic. An individual so labelled might almost be supposed to have an extra chromosome or personality trait which renders them more likely than the next person to cause harm in most or all situations. It also tends to infer a great many other qualities; impulsivity, deliberate destructiveness, a reckless indifference as to consequences and an imperviousness to punishment are all somehow conjured up in the powerful image of a dangerous person. *Yet many of those who commit serious acts of harm have none of these qualities.*

Apply the same method to the understanding of more commonplace events and it is clear that adjectives describing temperament are of limited practical use in predicting specific behaviours. Would scores on a 'talkativeness' scale among your family members be a reliable indicator of willingness to invite Jehovah's Witnesses in for a good chat? Or to make a speech in public? Would the person voted as most generous in your department also, by definition, be the most likely to tolerate being shortchanged by £10 in a shop? Of course not; you would

31

clearly expect those behaviours to depend on other far more specific factors; their interest in religious debate, vigilance or lack of assertiveness may be more reliable predictors.

A great deal of empirical knowledge exists on the forces which actually shape behaviour; how it is learned and unlearned, what increases and decreases it, and so on. Once the focus of assessment has been firmly fixed on the *behaviour* in question, rather than the type of person, useful theories and principles can begin to be applied.

DISTINGUISHES BETWEEN HARMFUL ACTS

It would make life a lot simpler if every person to be assessed presented only one significant risk, but the reality is often horribly complicated.

Case Example

A man with a long criminal history of violent assault (usually on the police), and a period of serious sexual abuse of his sons some 10 years previously, was referred for risk assessment by Social Services who were concerned about the potential for harm towards his new baby boy. He had suffered for many years from paranoid schizophrenia, and had spent several years in Special Hospital after attempts to prevent him running away from the local psychiatric hospital had resulted in repeated assaults on nursing staff.

A psychiatric risk assessment had recently been produced by a doctor who had treated him for many years. Her conclusion was that as his mental illness was currently better controlled than it had ever been, the risk of reoffending was low. It was a tribute to the professional integrity (and courage!) of the social worker involved that he was dissatisfied with this analysis of past offending and requested a second, 'non-mental illness' assessment.

All the documentation relating to medical history and past offending was tracked down, and discussed with medical colleagues. It became evident that the violent behaviour was the direct result of delusional drive; the man was convinced that a political conspiracy was behind murder attempts on his family, and he would arm himself against anticipated attacks. Assaults occurred when the police tried to take away the hammers and axes with which he escorted his

---

family to church, or when they entered his home to confiscate unauthorised firearms.

The sexual offending, on the other hand, *pre-dated* his mental illness. He was recorded as having developed the symptoms of schizophrenia some time into the sentence he served for abusing his children. If the illness had played any part in the abuse, it would have been at most a disinhibiting factor in the earliest stages of the condition, rather than a primary drive. At the time of interview, his relatively well-controlled illness was certainly still active enough to produce an equivalent disinhibition.

The violence and the sexual offending were therefore the results of two separate processes, and different factors would determine their risk of recurrence in the future. He was assessed as presenting a significant risk of sexual abuse of his son.

While a case may be complicated, therefore, in that more than one harmful behaviour is involved, when each is analysed individually the picture becomes clearer.

As will be seen in later chapters, it may be necessary to distinguish between different *contexts*, in which apparently similar behaviour occurs. Violence towards the police, for example, may well be the result of very different causal factors from those which influence physical abuse of children. Shoplifting and domestic burglary, which can occur together in a fairly undifferentiated, antisocial pattern for one person, may also point to sharply contrasting influences and functions in another individual.

Case Example

A 35 year old man with more than fifteen convictions for assault, affray and GBH was charged with attempted murder of his cohabitee. A casual glance at his criminal record would have suggested a pattern of habitual violence and poor controls, with a high degree of risk for future partners.

More detailed exploration of his earlier offences, however, revealed that they had occurred within a very narrow range of situations. The man had belonged to a motorcycle gang with a long-established custom of visiting local tourist towns on Bank Holidays. This attracted predictable antagonism from similar bands of youths; the enthusiastic battles which broke out between them were probably seen by all concerned as essential highlights of the holidays. Certainly, the victims of this man's assaults were usually themselves similarly charged, and police officers involved in the arrests had frequently expressed the view that the violence took place between consenting adults.

Interviews with the man's family and others established that he had been considered a mild-mannered figure at home. It transpired that he had tended to be dominated by his partner, to whom he was devoted, and whose numerous infidelities he had tolerated to an extent that most considered excessive. He had believed that she needed to 'have her fling', but that she would never leave him. When she eventually declared her intention to do so, taking their child with her, and all his attempts to prevent her failed, he apparently fell into clinical depression. It was after one of her short returns to him, at the point where she again announced that she was leaving, that the intensely violent attempt on her life occurred.

Clearly, his 'recreational' violence provided little insight into the factors which drove this desperate attack.

In the earlier case example of a man who had committed sexual assaults on both children and animals, some apparently *unconnected* behaviours were found on further analysis to be linked in an essential way. It is equally vital to establish whether or not seemingly *related* acts are in fact influenced by the same collection of factors.

FOUR

CONSIDERING PAST BEHAVIOUR

The best predictor of future behaviour is past behaviour.

EXPRESSED INTENTIONS by the assessed individual are usually far less reliable as indicators than their track record, but clinicians and other professionals tend to overvalue these accounts regardless. Perhaps this is not so surprising; the client is often certain that they will not repeat their harmful actions, and is likely to present as:

a. a reasonable person,
b. who shares the worker's perspective and values,
c. has been overwhelmed by environmental pressures, and
d. is effectively deterred by the prospect of future punishment.

The phrase 'too much to lose' regularly occurs. The empathic professional is likely to recognise the basic rationality of this position, identify with the client and consequently underestimate the future risk.

Of course, clients' evaluations may be completely accurate. It would be equally misguided, at the other end of the scale, to assume that they are members of an alien species whose own behaviour is beyond their understanding and control. In order to maintain a realistically balanced perspective, the following knowledge of the frequency and nature of the past behaviour is necessary.

HOW OFTEN HAS THE BEHAVIOUR OCCURRED BEFORE?

All other factors considered, the more often a behaviour occurs, the more likely it is to be repeated. A regular drinker tends to find it more difficult to give up than an occasional one; a parent who has frequently resorted to smacking his child will probably struggle to manage without physical punishment tactics compared with someone who has rarely smacked. Repeatedly violent offenders are known to become increasingly more likely to be reconvicted, while sexual offenders against children who have had several victims have been shown to be at higher risk of reoffending.

Some of the factors which may be implied in frequently repeated behaviour include *strength of drive, habit formation, limited response repertoires, poor controls* and *abnormal environments* (see later chapters).

OVER WHAT TIME PERIOD?

Where an action has been repeated often over a long period, especially with only short intervals between incidents, a greater probability of recurrence is usually indicated. Other factors are important to consider, however....

IN HOW WIDE A RANGE OF CIRCUMSTANCES HAS IT OCCURRED?

A person who develops a new internal state (eg mental illness, reaction to loss) and embarks on a concentrated burst of uncharacteristic behaviour is clearly at high risk of repeating it while their condition remains untreated; the probability reduces sharply afterwards. An example of this could be a person married happily for 20 years who suddenly becomes violent to their spouse while depressed. Similarly, external factors may be crucial. Someone who has had six previous cohabitees and has only been violent towards one is likely to be understood quite differently from a person violent to five or six.

The issues to be considered are the **unusualness** and the **specificity** of internal or external factors which seem to be necessary for the behaviour to occur. Where neither category of factors appears specific or unusual (in other words, when the behaviour arises in varied situations and states of mind), a more pervasive, long-standing vulnerability or drive may be indicated.

WHAT IS THE POPULATION BASE RATE?

This is the *ACTUARIAL* question; ie how often does this kind of behaviour occur in this group of individuals? As mentioned in Chapter 2, errors can be made if it is not known how common a behaviour is among the sub-population being considered. The base rate in question may be that of **the behaviour itself.** For instance, in predicting the likelihood of a violent assault on a prison officer by an inmate, the frequency of assaults on staff in that prison should be established. (If 65% of prisoners are known to have behaved in this way, the future probability of that individual doing so is clearly higher than chance, all else being equal).

Where two or more behaviours seem to be related (for example, assaults and drug taking among inmates), the base rate of the secondary one may also be significant. A teenage house burglar may be thought to be at even higher risk of reoffending when it is discovered that she has resumed her casual shoplifting; but how common is shoplifting among her non-burgling peers? Could it be that everyone in the neighbourhood steals from shops, but very few from houses? Has it actually been established in her case that her return to one crime increases the risk of the other, or is that assumption largely an indication of the assessor's different background and experience?

This distinction can prove crucial at a later point in a **continuing** assessment, where it is discovered that a minor 'deviant' activity or a possibly influential factor has re-emerged. A stable relationship, supposed to have been a steadying influence, might come to an end: non-violent bullying might start up: employment may be lost. What implication does this have in terms of the main risk? An understanding of the relevant base rates and a sound *formulation* (see Chapter 5) will prove invaluable in such circumstances.

HOW HAS THE BEHAVIOUR BEEN AFFECTED BY PAST PUNISHMENT?

While it is not usually as powerful as reward, punishment can be an extremely effective means of reducing undesirable behaviour or stopping it altogether. Everyone can probably recall having developed some regrettable habit (bullying, cheating in school, a risky driving practice) until a memorable event suddenly 'brought us to our senses'. The acceptable limits become starkly clear and the possible consequences of carrying on as before are now unthinkable.

For many offenders, the effects of initial discovery and public condemnation are punishing enough to reduce sharply any future risk-taking. Following the first arrest, different offences and groups of offenders are likely to have different *re-offence* and *re-*

conviction rates, and knowledge of these is an important starting point. Once you have established that, say, only 25% of the relevant group tend to behave in the same way again after their first (or fourth, or thirtieth) arrest, you can go on to examine evidence that your particular individual represents a higher or lower probability than the group average.

It is also useful to determine how severe or costly to that individual the previous punishment has been. Three probation orders may have had little effect on a young man's joyriding career, while the short prison sentence may have affected him far more deeply because of his own particular vulnerabilities. On the other hand, many who go on to reoffend may have *described* their earlier punishments as highly aversive while returning almost immediately to their old pattern of harmful behaviour; corroborative information from family members and friends will be useful in identifying any genuine effect.

Key questions about past behaviour include:

- *How often has the person acted in this way before?*
- *Over what time period? How regularly? With what intervals?*
- *In what range of circumstances?*
- *Are any actuarial statistics useful? eg the prevalence of the behaviour among other similar individuals, the likelihood of relapse or recidivism among that group etc.*
- *How has the behaviour been affected by punishment/other consequences in the past?*

FIVE

MOTIVATIONAL DRIVE

IT IS usually assumed that the forward drive or *motivation* to commit an act is the single most important factor necessary in understanding it. (Motivation is probably a more useful term than *motive*, which implies a conscious decision to act in pursuit of particular gains.) While not every case may be this straightforward, it will certainly be integral to any formulation to identify which of many possible motivations drives the behaviour.

It is when the motivation is in doubt that specialist assessment is most likely to be necessary. This will usually be psychological or psychiatric, although other opinions such as general medical, neurological, paediatric or psycho-pharmacological may also be relevant on occasion.

The need to identify the primary drive is recognised more readily in some cases than others. Most people would accept that shoplifting, for example, can arise from a number of drives other than the obvious material one of getting something for nothing. Depression, despair, boredom and anger may be far more significant than urgent need in driving the behaviour . On the other hand, burglars seem more likely to be viewed as purely acquisitive in motivation. This may be due in part to the more aggressive (as opposed to passive-aggressive and opportunistic) element of burglaries, which reduces the sympathy of the assessor and hence their inclination to look for other drives in the offender. Motivation in 'aggressors', whether sexual or otherwise, tends to be assumed rather than analysed, and the conclusions can be erroneously simplistic as a result.

At the other end of the scale, clients who induce empathy can often convince themselves and their assessors that the most obvious drive was absent altogether.

Case Example

Elderly men who sexually abuse youngsters while under enormous pressures themselves may well attribute this uncharacteristic behaviour to trauma and stress alone. One such man, recently widowed after nursing his wife through a long illness, was described by his probation officer as having 'absolutely no sexual motive' for the minor but repeated acts of indecency on his great-niece.

Following in-depth psychosexual assessment, which revealed an intensifying pattern of deviant sexual fantasy and offence planning, the case was discussed among the team. It transpired that the probation officer's comments were based on her belief that the man presented a low risk of re-offending, a conclusion shared by her team colleagues. She was also accurate in highlighting the importance of non-sexual drives, loneliness and grief, behind his actions. However, it was not useful to the offender nor to his victim to deny the very real sexual component, which formed a central part of the relapse prevention and reconciliation work still to be done.

Those who have themselves been the victims of others' abuse are also likely to have their own motivational drive misattributed. There is no natural law stating that victims cannot be active (as well as reactive) victimisers, but some groups of previously abused or disadvantaged individuals tend to be viewed in a more sympathetic light than others, as if their own sufferings justify their subsequent behaviour. An abusive mother who as a child experienced well-documented sexual violence from her father may be described as 'responding to traumatic and impoverished parenting models', while her male counterpart may find his own claim of childhood abuse dismissed as 'shifting the blame for his actions onto others':

> The **responsibility** for an act, which rests solely on the perpetrator, should never be confused with **influences** on it, however valid and powerful they may be.

It is not only in the assessment stage that a clear understanding of the motivation is essential. Intervention based on an erroneous formulation runs the risk of being at best, ineffectual and at worst, positively harmful.

Case Example

It is generally recognised that sexual offenders often have a limited ability to empathise with their victims. They can misinterpret friendly behaviour as sexually invitational, or passive resistance as cooperation. 'Victim Empathy' work has therefore become an integral part of sex offender programmes, and is sometimes undertaken automatically by those with little experience in this sort of work, on the grounds that nothing else would otherwise be provided, and that if it does not benefit every offender, it can at least do no harm.

Unfortunately, this is just not be the case. One type of sexual offender is motivated primarily by a sadistic drive, in which sexual arousal is related to the suffering of the victim. Increasing awareness of the suffering is likely to feed deviant fantasy and *increase* the probability of future offending.

Another type of child abuser typically has a marked lack of social confidence, which often triggers in helping professionals a bout of social skills training. The reasoning tends to be that if 'empowered' in adult interactions, the offender will form non-deviant relationships. If this is applied to an abuser who is both socially inept *and* primarily aroused by children, however, the result will be a far more efficient molester.

A basic principle in assessing motivation, therefore is: *just because a person with an unusual characteristic or circumstances also behaves harmfully, it does not follow that the one caused the other*.

Issues to be addressed in identifying motivation should include the following.

IS THERE A SIGNIFICANT MENTAL ILLNESS FACTOR?

It is not sufficient to ask whether the client suffers from a mental illness (or any other type); most of the actions of a mentally ill person are the result of non-illness factors. Rather:

- Was the person behaving in a way *uncharacteristic* of them when well?
- Is there strong evidence that illness was a *sufficient, necessary* or *significant* part of the motivational drive?

- Were they perhaps *predisposed* towards this behaviour by the mood or thinking known to be a function of the illness?— At the very least, is it possible that the illness had a *disinhibiting* effect, in that it weakened their normal controls?

A psychiatric assessment will be necessary to establish such facts, although in practice, the decision to seek a psychiatric opinion will frequently be taken by non-medical professionals. If there is no multiprofessional team to offer this sort of screening, therefore, it is important to have a good general awareness of the indicators which should prompt a psychiatric or medical referral.

When the behaviour in question occurred at some time in the past, and it is claimed that this took place as a result of or at least during a period of mental/emotional disturbance, this needs to be verified.

> ### Case Example
> A businessman charged with setting fire to his shop reported that this had happened when he was extremely depressed and receiving psychiatric treatment. His family confirmed the depressed episode and were able to produce appointment cards predating the offences in support of this. However, when the psychiatrist in question was contacted and checked his records, it transpired that the early appointments concerned the man's minor anxieties about his sexual potency, while the first mention of the severe depression occurred the week *after* his arrest. It seemed that he had subsequently managed to convince his family (and possibly himself) that events had occurred in a rather different order.

Psychiatrists and physicians may also be able to identify the presence of medical symptoms in individuals not otherwise considered ill or mentally disturbed; (for example, subtle mannerisms or physical characteristics may suggest a organic disease process, brain damage or the toxic effects of drugs). Such underlying pathology seems to be most commonly overlooked in individuals who (a) already have a history of conspicuous and/or psychosomatic complaints, or (b) lead eccentric or deviant lifestyles which they clearly enjoy.

WHAT IS THE INFLUENCE OF PREVIOUS LEARNING ON THE BEHAVIOUR?

In a behavioural analysis, the term *antecedents* refers to those events in the individual's past which have significance in their present actions. These events can be *long past* (distal antecedents) such as childhood experiences, or *more recent* (proximal antecedents) such as a marital relationship. The experience may have been *subjectively positive* (eg enjoyable sexual contact) or *negative* (eg separation), and sometimes both (eg where childhood illness leads to greater intimacy with a parent). The learning may have occurred through *direct means* such as teaching or personal experience, or *indirectly* from important role models. It may have happened as a result of *one significant episode* (eg personal injury) or over *a sustained period* (eg taking on a premature adult role in the family).

In all cases, and in childhood experiences particularly, it is important to understand the individual's perception of events *at the time they occurred*, rather than their current view or feelings. Behaviours are often powerfully ingrained at a time when a child experiences the world simply but intensely, when superficial incidents can take on all-or-nothing importance and when the repertoire of responses is limited. Even when, as an adult, the individual has more control over events and more strategic options, the influence of the earlier learning may cause them to re-experience the intense emotions of childhood and encourage them to act in similar ways. The degree of insight and control retained over such feelings and behaviour will vary between individuals and often between situations.

Case Example

A young woman was facing charges of criminal damage and threats to kill, having carried out a vendetta against an ex-boyfriend when their short and quite casual relationship ended. At interview, it transpired that she had acted in a similarly extreme way once before, but was in general able to accept the breakdown of relationships quite rationally and had in fact ended several herself.

In taking her history, it emerged that her mother had died when she was 3 years old, and that she had been brought up by her father, a rather distant and emotionally cold man. He worked long, irregular hours and she recalled spending much of her childhood and adolescence alone in the house, which she learned to accept passively, learning that he found conflict distressing. When she was 12, however, he became involved with a another woman and did not tell his daughter, but withdrew even further emotionally and began to spend most nights away. Neighbours informed Social Services and one day the girl was taken from school into care, without warning and in great distress. Her father made only half-hearted contact for a few months and then disappeared from her life. Her passive acceptance of his neglect, which she had believed would ensure his continued presence had failed her.

Years later, the two men from whom she was unable to separate were also very cool and indifferent towards her. Normally self-sufficient, she found herself developing an intense dependency on them almost immediately, and making excessive demands which alarmed and soon alienated them completely. She herself had been unaware of the parallels between her childhood and adult experiences, and of her own role in re-creating situations of powerlessness and rejection.

WHAT WERE THE NECESSARY CONDITIONS/TRIGGERS AT THE TIME?

Antecedents also include events which closely preceded the behaviour. These may be *internal* (eg emotions, thoughts, arousal) or *external* (eg situations, actions of others), and will exert varying degrees of influence.

Almost everyone is capable of committing any harmful action; deliberately killing another person, for instance. A few are already so strongly predisposed towards the act that it takes very little to push them over the edge. Most of us probably believe that the circumstances would have to be extraordinary (defending our families, a state of war etc) to drive us to such extremes. As discussed in a previous chapter, it is to be expected that the person concerned will tend to emphasise the importance of *external* events in bringing about their behaviour. The professional, on the other hand, will be trying to establish the relative influence of both individual (internal) and environmental (external) factors. It is difficult to imagine a behaviour falling at the absolute ends of this range; almost all our actions come somewhere in between, being dependent on both sources of influence.

100%	100%
Internally	Externally
Driven	Driven

When a person has exhibited similar harmful acts on a number of occasions, it is important to identify what those situations had in common. Significant environmental features may include the setting, background stressors, the presence and conduct of other people including the victim, and expectations and demands made on the individual (according to their perception, or that of others).

Also important are *absent* factors; significant people who are not around, demands which do not occur, and the relaxation or failure of normal constraints and boundaries.

Case Example

A young man with a long history of violence towards male peers in pubs was unable to identify any necessary conditions other than the presence of suitable adversaries. He had attacked smaller and larger men, acquaintances and strangers, with provocation and without, drunk or sober. He expressed considerable pride in his pugnacious reputation, and his only motivation to change was based on the fact that his closest friends were beginning to reject him.

He was asked to draw up a record of recent incidents including details of all the external and internal factors known to influence different types of violence. Only two necessary conditions emerged; his mother had to be absent and his cousin, generally felt to be a good influence on him, had to be present. On further investigation he was able to identify a vague but powerful sense of decorum when in his mother's company, and a reassuring belief that his more stable cousin could extricate him from any difficulties caused by his own violence.

This modest insight formed the basis for therapeutic success according to his own aims; he managed to restrict his assaultative behaviour to a level acceptable to his family and friends (if not to wider social norms!)

Substance use/abuse is sometimes considered to be an external factor, sometimes internal. While clearly an artificial addition to the individual's natural state, it is equally something that they themselves choose to introduce to the situation, rather than an attribute of the situation itself. It will be considered in greater depth in the next chapter, in terms of its effect on the individual's normal controls.

... and why it isn't always obvious

Put simply, in order for behaviour to occur, there needs to be a prospect of some benefit. For it to recur, something must have rewarded, or *reinforced* it. We go to work because we get paid for it, because it brings satisfaction, or maybe because people are nicer to us there than they are at home. We drink because we like the taste, or for the relaxing effect. We are nice to others because it makes us feel good and reassures us that they will be nice to us in turn.

This is not to say that the individual is necessarily aware of the most powerful reinforcers, nor that they subjectively *feel* rewarded in a pleasurable way. In fact, the only reliable definition of reinforcement is: *the result of an action which increases the probability of that action happening again.* Sometimes, a consequence which appears at face value to be a reinforcement for behaviour actually turns out to be quite the reverse. For example, we would normally accept that payment acts as a reward. Imagine, however, the effect on your dignified elderly neighbour who has done you the favour of mowing your stretch of grass verge as well as his own, of having a fiver pressed into his hand! He may well be dreadfully embarrassed, feel that his kind gesture has been misread, and be inhibited from repeating it ever again. In effect, if not in intent, your response has been a *punishing* one, because it has reduced the probability of the behaviour recurring.

The reverse can also be true, in that *consequences which are intended to be discouraging, or may be experienced as aversive, sometimes reinforce behaviour.* A child who finds it difficult to win much positive response from her parents when she is behaving well is likely to find even an angry reaction more rewarding than indifference, even while it superficially distresses her. Flirtatious behaviour by one partner may be reinforced by the aggressively jealous reactions of their spouse who cannot express affection any other way.

Offending behaviour naturally carries the threat of significant cost to the offender, whether legal, social or emotional. We know that for the offence to be repeated, *the reinforcement must exceed the punishment experienced*, but it is often difficult to see how.

Frequently, the answer lies in the powerful effect of *immediacy*. A reward (or punishment) following instantly on the act tends to be have far more effect on subsequent behaviour than a delayed one, as anyone who has house-trained a pet will know well. As for humans, one of the benefits of growing up is that we tend to be influenced more and more by long-term consequences rather than immediate gain. On the brink of a delicious temptation or of a tedious duty, it is (usually) possible to push away thoughts of how good the next five minutes *could* be, and focus on the ultimate goal, wider principles and potential repercussions. People who have not developed this ability, or whose normal controls are weakened by circumstances, are likely to be overwhelmed by the prospect of *immediate gratification*.

When a number of obvious rewards for a behaviour have been identified, and still seem inadequate to outweigh the punishment, it is often useful to ask:

> *'How would it be if, at that moment, in that situation, you* didn't *behave like this?'*

The answer may be 'I'd feel like a rotten mother', 'I'd think my mates despised me', 'I'd still be left with the craving': in other words, the feeling would be intolerable.

Case Example

It was clear that a young car thief gained status among his peers, a sense of control and excitement from his offending. However, this did not seem sufficient to outweigh the negative consequences of arrest and detention, particularly his family's distress, which obviously upset him greatly.

On further exploration, it emerged that the boy's mother had recently remarried, and that he felt sharply deposed from his position as head of the household. The achievements of which he had been proud, (his academic success, physical strength and male protectiveness), had all been completely eclipsed by his stepfather's greater abilities.

He had then discovered a deviant means of regaining much of his self-image. The absolute gains were modest, and just allowed him to maintain self-respect. The alternative, however, was to return to the state of painful limbo and loss where he counted for nothing, and this was intolerable.

This is the principle of *negative reinforcement*, which does not mean punishment, as some believe, but rather the rewarding effect of *relief from an aversive experience*. (One way of remembering this is that negative reinforcement is like hitting your head against a brick wall, it's so nice when it stops)

Sometimes the behaviour itself causes both the discomfort and the relief. In the case of an addiction or dependency, for example, abstinence tends to cause a build up of tension and other discomfort, which can be relieved by indulging in the behaviour again. (A recent study of smoking found that smokers do suffer higher levels of stress than non-smokers, but that most of the stress results from withdrawal from the last cigarette.) Even a non-substance habit like watching the television, having a regular quiet time or taking risks can lead to physical and psychological discomfort if interrupted for too long, and powerful negative reinforcement when it is restarted. It is probably fair to say that *relief* from anxiety, boredom or discomfort is one of the most powerful reinforcers for behaviour.

Other common behaviours which are reinforced because they relieve anxiety include distraction (eg getting engrossed in some trivial activity), disruption (eg creating a diversion), risk-taking, avoidance (eg running away), anger and violence (which can reduce helpless feelings under threat) and self harm (as an alternative to unacceptable anger). Many of these can become habit-forming and the original cause of anxiety left far behind. The reinforcement has then become *internalised* (ie it makes you feel better, although nothing has changed) and the behaviour *generalised* to new situations where it is inappropriate or ineffective.

IS THERE EVIDENCE OF A DEVIANT DRIVE?

A vital question to be addressed when considering harmful behaviour is *whether the motivational drive itself is deviant* (that is, unusually harmful), or just *the means by which it is being achieved*. A normally gentle mother at the end of her tether who smacks her perpetually crying baby may cause as much harm as one who derives enjoyment from physical chastisement, but the motivational drive and future risk may be very different. The desire to stop a baby crying is not in itself deviant or harmful, although the desperate means employed by the first woman clearly caused suffering. The need to bring about instant obedience in a tiny infant through punishment is certainly more abnormal, and could suggest a sadistic drive or an excessive need for absolute control. Whereas in the first example, risk may be reduced by providing practical support or training in child management techniques, the second would probably require more intensive psychological therapy, always assuming that there was sufficient motivation to change at all.

It is not always a simple matter to disentangle the drive from the means of achieving it. Most if not all needs and desires probably start out normally if you trace them back far enough. Sometimes, however, the maladaptive behaviour has been learned in such a powerful way, or at such an impressionable time, or has gone on so long, that the drive has become inextricably bound to it.

Case Example

An inadequate and isolated youth was so painfully shy that he found it impossible to talk to girls, although his overwhelming desire was to develop a close and intimate relationship. Over a number of years, he made a few clumsy attempts at friendship and received humiliating rejections in the process. He gradually developed fantasies in which he kidnapped women and forced them into sexual encounters, during which they recognised his true worth and became devoted to him in return. By the time he was 30, he was enacting these fantasies in horrific assaults.

After a number of rapes, interspersed with prison sentences, he began psychosexual therapy. Although he still expressed the belief that his ideal was a non-coercive sexual relationship, it soon became clear that he was now only aroused by violent sex, and that degradation of his victim was the central focus of his fantasies. The original desire for sexual intimacy had become part of a now primary deviant drive.

Where confusion arises between original needs and a learned maladaptive behaviour, it may be useful to ask:

- What alternative means exist for this individual to achieve the same ends?
- How able are they to make use of these? *and*
- How intellectually aware are they of the costs of their actions?

It will be important in some cases to establish the extent to which the client actually *understands the harmfulness or illegality of the behaviour* in question, as well as whether they have the resources or opportunity to use alternatives.

It may be useful to plot both the normality/deviance of the

drive together with the internal/external nature of the influences on it.

	Normal	
x A		*x* C
Internal		External
x B		*x* D
	Deviant	

Behaviour A is the result of normal, internal drives; an example could be an unpopular person stealing in order to give presents to would-be friends.

Behaviour B is deviantly and internally driven; for instance someone who derives pleasure from torturing animals.

Behaviour C is the result of a normal, externally influenced drive; for example an assault, to prevent a loved one from leaving them by a dependent person.

Behaviour D would be deviantly but externally driven; such as an individual with a propensity to violence battering a child who won't stop crying.

In general (though there are many exceptions), harmful behaviours which are the result of normal drives or externally triggered tend to be more amenable to change: those deviantly and/or internally driven are more likely to recur.

Key questions about motivational drive include:

- *Is mental illness, or a particular mental state, significant?*
- *How important are early learning experiences?*
- *To what extent is the behaviour triggered by other events?*
- *What consequences reinforce the behaviour?*
- *Is there evidence of a deviant drive, or of a normal drive satisfied by deviant means?*
- *Does the research indicate any recognised drives which correspond to this behaviour?*

SIX

CONTROLS AND DISINHIBITORS

WHAT SEPARATES those who commit offences from those who do not?

Last time you went shopping in a supermarket or large department store, the chances are that at the same time, someone else was there stealing something. What reasons might they have given for their behaviour?

- They wanted the item badly; it would go well in their house (....you liked it even more, having collected many similar ones).
- They could not really afford it (....they had more in their bank account than you did at that moment).
- They had had a deprived childhood (....no more so than many other people in the store).
- They were under stress, having three children under five at home (....so had you, in the past).
- Their partner was currently threatened with redundancy (....yours once *was* made redundant).

So what accounts for the shoplifting? Theirs are fairly commonplace circumstances and feelings. Perhaps it is more useful to ask 'Why didn't *you* steal?' What intervened, in your case, between the motivation and the act?

An important advance in the sexual offending field in recent decades has been the penile plethysmograph (PPG), an instrument which measures and records physiological male sexual arousal. Those first hearing about this new device perhaps imagined that it represented a breakthrough in distinguishing those who had committed sexual offences but were denying it, from those who were falsely accused. Surely all suspects could now be connected to the PPG, shown deviant stimulus material (children, rape scenes etc) and hey presto! Those who were guilty would instantly give themselves away by becoming aroused, while those who did not would be innocent.

Of course, it wasn't that simple. Researchers went on to seek out normative data, not only on confirmed sexual offenders and denying suspects, but also on *the non-offending population*. Through such work it has been established, for example, that at least 60% of men can become aroused by children (ie those under the age of 16) in some circumstances. Far from being a hallmark of the 'dangerous pervert', it seems that the presence of such arousal is actually more normal (statistically) than is its absence. Only *acting* on the arousal is abnormal. Similarly, while arousal to scenes of sexual violence is often (but not always) found in those who rape, it is also common in those who do not, and so on.

(Incidentally, while the procedure for measuring female sexual arousal exists, it is not used routinely in Britain. However, there is reason to expect that similar arousal patterns would emerge.)

It is evident from these examples, then, that the *motivation* to commit a harmful act is not in itself sufficient to predict who will and who will not *actually* commit it, nor is it an adequate *explanation* for the behaviour when it happens. One also needs to ask: 'Why them?' 'Why this?' 'Why now?' If the individual has rarely or never behaved in this way before, or if the frequency of the behaviour has risen sharply, then either their motivational drive has increased significantly, or *their controls have diminished*.

There are a number of aspects to be considered when assessing a person's control, and what strengthens or weakens it. Some of the more important ones are considered here.

EXISTING MORAL CODE

As a starting point, it is useful to establish how well-developed is the assessed person's moral framework. Do they recognise that a particular action was wrong, for instance, or do they merely consider it punishable? For example, a young woman who believes that smoking cannabis is a valid, justifiable means of relaxing presents a different picture of likely future behaviour from one who feels that she has developed a undesirable and harmful habit under pressure of circumstances.

If the individual comes from a cultural or subcultural background quite different from that of the assessor, it will be necessary to establish whether their relevant moral values are also those of their group. Of course, this does not alter the fact that the behaviour is illegal and/or harmful, but it may allow a more complete understanding of the efficiency of their controls, as well as the motivational drive and level of any deviance.

Case Example

In a New Zealand secure unit, a Maori in-patient who suffered from schizophrenia had also been convicted of sexual offences against children. At a time when his psychosis was felt to be well-controlled, he told his doctor that adult-child sexual behaviour was encouraged in his tribal group as an educational principle.

The clinical team contacted one of the tribal elders, who attended the next case conference and provided detailed information about the child-rearing principles of the group. While there were significant differences between Maori and European-derived views on nudity, acceptable physical proximity and other conduct within the family, the strong taboo against adult-child sex was shared by both cultures. Later, the elder confronted the patient, challenging his statement and saying 'That was a terrible thing to say about our people. You know perfectly well how we all feel about what you have done. What would your mother say if she could hear you?' The man appeared ashamed and admitted that he had hoped to deceive the clinical team, knowing the respect they had for Maori culture.

Another individual exhibiting anti-social behaviour may be discovered to share this activity with the majority of people in their extended family, neighbourhood or identified sub-/culture. In such a case, it will be important to determine the individual's recognition of the illegality and/or harmfulness of their actions as well as their ability to distance themselves from group norms.

It is not only the assessed person's moral position on the *key* behaviour which may be significant. Some individuals clearly have strong principles which guide their conduct in every other area of life, but have somehow missed, blurred or undermined those relating to the relevant behaviour. Others have a poor moral grasp in general, perhaps as a result of more general intellectual deficits, or through faulty learning or emotional/ psychiatric disturbance. As a general rule, (and taking into account the strength of deviant drive) it seems to be easier to generate or re-establish effective codes for the key behaviour where a well-functioning moral system already exists in other areas of the person's life. They will tend to need less convincing that working towards greater control is in their best interests, and have a greater sense of *self-efficacy*, or belief that they can achieve it.

For those with little or no appreciation of right and wrong as it applies to the crucial issues, their proven ability to *adhere to rules reinforced by the prospect of punishment* will be a primary consideration in assessing future risk.

EMPATHY WITH VICTIM

For most people, it seems that 'fellow feeling' for the object of their actions is a powerful factor in self-control. Moral training in childhood often involves invocation of empathy, (eg 'How would you feel if someone did that to you?'), and this is often linked to an awareness of social acceptability (eg 'What would people think of you if they knew what you were doing?')

It is often assumed that those who have been the victims of harmful treatment will have a greater empathy with those who suffer similarly. While this does often follow, we are all aware of cases where the opposite applies; an example is the over-punitive parent who argues 'My mother thrashed me regularly when I deserved it, and it never did me any harm'. It seems that some people learn from traumatic experiences to identify with the stronger party, and to distance themselves from the victim's suffering. This does not necessarily lead to re-enactment, of course; many will merely feel uncomfortable, unsympathetic or critical when they encounter victimisation again.

A number of victims do go on to inflict on weaker individuals abuse similar to that which they experienced themselves. Some may believe consciously that the treatment is justified, as in the last example. Others may try to act differently, but find that uncertainty and anxiety (for example, about issues of control) are powerfully relieved by falling back on familiar patterns of behaviour. They may develop new attitudes which support their actions (eg 'I'm not the sadistic brute my father was, but these children only respond to a firm hand'). Another group remain painfully aware that they are replicating their own abuse, but have failed in all their attempts to establish a new pattern.

> ### Case Example
> One young man expressed intense distress over his numerous domestic burglaries, recalling vividly his own sense of helpless grief and outrage when he and his mother had suffered similarly in his childhood. After his parents' separation, his father and his friends had repeatedly broken into their house at night to steal and damage their possessions. At the same time, every weekend the boy would be taken to stay at his father's new home, where he would see the stolen articles displayed. Terrified that he would lose all contact with the father he still loved, he tried to ignore the evidence and said nothing. After the visits, he denied to his mother that his father had the property, and felt that he was betraying both her and himself in doing so.
>
> He found in time that desecrating others' homes relieved some of the intolerable conflict which he had experienced as the 'knowing victim', but he never lost his intense feelings of identification with those he violated through his burglaries.

Clearly, not all those who commit harmful acts have themselves been brutalised. Even so, their capacity for empathy with their victims will vary, and needs to be understood.

Where false 'rationalisations', or flawed but internally logical reasons about the victim have been developed to explain the behaviour, it is useful to explore these further. Is the individual well aware, for example, that they chose to see the victim in this light *after* the behaviour had already been conceived? Or do they genuinely believe that their own actions have been caused or justified by those of the victim? As will be discussed later (Chapter 10), the victim may indeed have exerted some influence, and if so this needs to be acknowledged. Other factors in the relationship, however brief, will benefit from closer scrutiny. Motives may have been misread (sometimes genuinely but often as a reflection of the need of the offender); innocuous actions may have been experienced as triggers for powerful emotions or desires.

Many offenders may feel that to admit to *any* awareness of the victim's suffering will portray them as a monster, and they will naturally resist attracting such a label. Far from understanding that a lack of expressed empathy presents a more worrying picture, they may believe that this is the most benign way to portray their actions ('If I'd had any idea that she found it distressing, I'd never have dreamed...'). For this and many other reasons, it is therefore crucial to create a non-threatening atmosphere for the assessment, in which the individual is encouraged to express both the awareness of suffering and the irresistible drive to proceed with the behaviour, if that is an accurate description of events as they saw them. It will then be possible for the assessor to gauge the extent or absence of empathy, the potential for its development, and its relative importance in future risk.

INCONGRUENCE WITH SELF-IMAGE

Where a particular behaviour is sharply at odds with the way a person perceives themselves, there are often stronger inhibitions against it. Conversely, if an otherwise undesirable act is somehow consistent with a major part of the self-image, controls against it are likely to be weaker.

Think about your own profession or team: although breaking the law is generally condemned, some offences may in practice be more acceptable than others. Speeding convictions and parking tickets are seen in some circles as occupational hazards; in fields which prize risk-taking and tough-mindedness, a clean licence may actually hint at a lack of commitment ! Similarly, perfectly respectable professionals may feel that admissions of drug-taking back in their student days, nights in the cells after stag-night revelries or minor public order offences during political demonstrations would do nothing to diminish their reputations in the eyes of their colleagues. Few however would feel that sexual or violent offences against vulnerable individuals, for example, were compatible with their professional or personal image.

It is important, therefore, in assessing risk, to understand the extent to which harmful behaviour has been perceived by the individual as consistent (or discordant) with their view of themselves.

In cases where the harmful behaviour seems entirely at odds with the usual behaviour and character of the individual, it is often difficult to understand its attraction, particularly in view of the risks involved. Frequently the answer can be found in the **function** of the behaviour in restoring or enhancing some threatened aspect of the person's self-image. Many people whose lifestyles offer few legitimate opportunities for challenge may relish skilful risk-taking as a supplement. This may involve pot-holing or banger-racing...or credit card fraud. Those who feel that their sense of identity depends heavily on their sexual success, when deprived of appropriate outlets may find their normal controls against illegal sex weakened. In some cases, behaviours such as masturbation or extra-marital affairs, which could otherwise have reduced their frustration, may be regarded as **incompatible** with their self-image. An inadequate man, for example, may perceive masturbation as an unacceptable admission of failure to achieve a 'normal' sexual relationship.

Case Example

A young man of limited intelligence and little social confidence had been impressed by his peers' bragging about daring exploits. He learned that he could achieve a fragile acceptance by the group through dramatic, risk-taking behaviour, which escalated over time. Not recognising that the others viewed him with more amusement than respect, he eagerly took the stooge's role in joy-riding and vandalism sprees, for which he was frequently the only one caught. Far from having a punishing effect, the negative consequences were an additional source of pride to him; he began to adopt the dress and mannerisms of film and TV anti-heroes to an unusual degree. By the time his friends grew tired of him, it was clear that he had extended his anti-social conduct into his relationships with his family, who were far less tolerant of it and close to rejecting him.

In assessment, it became clear that he could conceive of no other mode of behaving which could provide anything like the satisfaction he had achieved in his days of glory with the gang. Impulsive risk-taking had become powerfully associated with excitement, popularity and self-respect, whereas his life before that period had been characterised by isolation and painful self-consciousness. Given its central position in his narrow self-image, and the lack of viable alternatives, it was highly unlikely that he would be able to curb the behaviour in the foreseeable future.

COGNITIVE DISTORTION

It is often difficult for the individual to recognise or acknowledge ways in which they managed to justify their harmful conduct at the time. Some harmful behaviours will have evolved quite gradually from ordinary or at least tolerated ones, with little conscious awareness of the point at which they crossed the boundaries of acceptability. Others will have been recognised as undesirable and regretted immediately, but continued perhaps because they went largely unpunished in relation to the benefits gained.

By the time they have been detected and confronted publicly with their behaviour, the person is often viewing it with stark clarity and regret. It is useful at this point to identify ways in which they managed to avoid seeing it in this way before; future risk may depend upon the degree to which those distortions still apply or could return in similar situations. Some of the more common ones are described here.

Redefining meaning of behaviour

It is common to blur vital distinctions such as harmful/harmless or legal/illegal, and to substitute hopeful euphemisms. 'I wasn't doing something wrong myself, I was just helping her out', 'Nobody else wanted it', 'It was just a bit of fun', 'I was ridding society of an evil' and 'I just loved them too much' would all be examples of this form of distortion.

Case Example
A young man who had been homosexually abused in his childhood went on to molest his five year old daughter while he was suffering from clinical depression. He described how he had blamed his own experience of abuse for his later homosexual prostitution, which he despised. When depressed, he had convinced himself that his daughter's first sexual contact needed to be heterosexual, and in the context of a loving relationship, if she were to develop a normal sexual orientation. He had hoped that, so influenced, she would go on to initiate her younger brother into similarly appropriate sexual patterns.

Undervaluing cost

Many people continue their redefinition by distorting the severity of the effect of their actions. The distortion may apply to the likely consequences to themselves; 'I'll never be caught', 'For such a minor offence, I thought I'd get off with a caution', or 'No-one bothers about possession of a little bit of cannabis these days; they're after the dealers'. This comfortable self-deceit is of course likely to have been shattered by subsequent exposure to reality.

In other cases, the distortion may apply to the cost to the victim, as in the 'spoilt goods' rationalisation (ie 'She was already sexually experienced, so what more harm could I do?'), or in the form of comparisons; (eg 'They had so much; they would never miss it'). As noted earlier, assessment should take account of the extent to which the distortion is shared among family, peer group or sub-culture, in order to identify the level of deviation from accepted norms. It will also be important to explore how much the individual's view has really changed since detection, or whether they are now only repeating the sentiments they feel are required of them.

Underestimating strength of drive

If an individual fails to recognise the most powerful influences driving their behaviour, they are less likely to adopt the most effective measures to control it. This will be covered more fully in the next chapter.

Misjudging others' reactions

Frequently, the perpetrator of harmful acts misjudges the views that others have of such behaviour.

Case Example

A young man had been arrested for battering to death an unpopular local itinerant. The victim was the focus for particular resentment locally at the time of the assault, as it was suspected that he had informed to the police on the criminal activities of other youngsters. His attacker had heard many of his friends threatening to 'kill' the man, and when his opportunity arose, felt that he was acting on their behalf for the general good. He was genuinely bewildered when he found that his actions were condemned by those with whom he felt he had shared a common intention.

Some very different behaviours are often carried out with the similar aim of gaining sympathy or increased support, but again have the opposite effect: self-harm is a common example. It could be that in the early development of the behaviour, it did indeed bring about the desired result. It then continues, increasing in severity and desperation, long after it has served to alienate the very people it sought to draw closer.

In other types of behaviour, and particularly in sexual offences, it is the attitude or feelings of the victim which are distorted. This may be necessary in order to over-ride a natural repugnance for brutality, or in order to maintain an acceptable self-image. Thus a rapist may see his victim as 'asking for it', not in the sense of deserving punishment, but as a willing participant who prefers not to give too obvious consent. The individual may find it only too easy to project their own desires onto others, or to allow their own excitement to blind them to the moment at which others no longer wish to participate. Harmful group activities can occur when no single member really wants to go further, but is afraid to object, believing that all the others are determined to continue.

Again, the extent to which the individual has regained a realistic perspective on others' views or feelings will be important in the assessment of future risk. Where the distortion is genuinely widely shared, and few appropriate values have been available in the person's experience, it may be useful to refer to the Motivational Model described in the final chapter.

IMPULSIVITY

This is a term frequently employed, but seldom correctly. It is often wrongly used to explain behaviours which contradict the intentions *declared* by the individual concerned; for example when an offender tells his therapist that he sincerely wants to stop offending, and then goes on to commit the same crime the next day (or on his way home from the session).

The tendency to behave impulsively for immediate gain, regardless of longer term consequences, is an extremely important factor in risk assessment. However, it is first necessary to determine whether this is an *enduring, generalised characteristic* of the individual's personality, or *a component of a specific habit*. Many people might be erroneously labelled as impulsive when in fact they lack control only in a particular situation, or in relation to a certain behaviour.

It is part of the definition of a *dependency*, or addictive behaviour, for example, that ability to resist repeating the behaviour is significantly impaired, even at great cost. It is not necessarily the case, however, that such a person will have impaired controls in another area of life. A compulsive gambler might be prone to break all good intentions and blow the rent money on another bingo session, but at the same time scrupulously observe their religious commitments. Someone with a severe tranquilliser dependency, who regularly lapses from a planned reduction programme and takes their week's prescription in the first two days, may have no difficulty in sticking to a strict diet. In these examples, the impulsiveness is an *encapsulated* behavioural phenomenon, which may have little bearing on the harmful conduct at the centre of the risk assessment.

In other cases, however, impulsivity may be a *personality trait*, an enduring characteristic of the individual which permeates most levels of their functioning. It may be evident that the person tends to act spontaneously, reckless as to the serious consequences of their actions, across a variety of behaviours and situations. Typically, their moral values and intellectual powers of decision-making are swamped at the crucial moment, usually by *emotional or ego-centric override*. This characteristic appears to be a significant indicator of future risk of harm, particularly where is seems that past punishment and skilled attempts at intervention have failed.

It cannot be assumed, however, that everyone who embarks regularly on ill-judged, self-defeating patterns of behaviour is simply impulsive, nor that the tendency will be resistant to change. As reiterated throughout this book, it is important to understand the *mechanism* behind a label, and to extend assessment into *an evaluation of ability to change*. Where your skills as a practitioner fall short of such an analysis, make this clear, and indicate the need for a more specialist involvement.

EMOTIONAL/EGOCENTRIC OVERRIDE

Many individuals who have caused considerable harm to others are able to describe entirely appropriate values and standards for behaviour, which would appear to be utterly inconsistent with their actual conduct. (This is not particularly unusual; most of us would probably advocate certain principles, say, for childrearing, alcohol consumption, and professional practice, which we are uncomfortably aware we have violated repeatedly in our own lives.) The dramatic difference is in the *degree* to which these individuals' standards differ from their behaviour. A father who can hold forth eloquently on his children's needs for protection and dignity can at the same time be physically abusing them on a regular basis. A mother who states forcefully the importance of providing a stable home for her child can miss successive contact meetings because of 'other commitments'; urgent minor demands which appear to take precedence over the long-term needs of the child.

What intervenes, between the good intention and the act, is often a powerful emotional need. Many people have learned consistently through their early lives that others' promises are unreliable, that opportunities to secure what is necessary must be taken whenever they arise. Others are painfully aware that in order to demonstrate dependence and loyalty, they are expected to act immediately to challenges or threats, or lose valuable support. Many are taught that restraint is weakness; that to deny oneself for another's sake is to play into the hands of the oppressors, whoever they may be. These are all variants on *emotional* over-drive; the sudden drive to behave in one's short-term interests, regardless of general principles. The *egocentric* variant, with which we are all familiar in its lesser forms, dictates that the individual violates normal rules because, at that moment, such a special person is above ordinary constraints.

For those well-adjusted souls who are able to keep long-term goals always in their sights, who *always* measure the importance of immediate demands carefully against the absolute priorities, such inconsistent behaviour from clients can indicate 'insufficient motivation' or 'lip service to acceptable conduct'. It is far more than that, of course, this vacillation between the ideal and the achieved behaviour. For many people, their high standard continues to be the benchmark against which they judge themselves; it proves that they are decent people, in comparison with those whose values are sloppy or downright immoral. It is in many ways their *strength* that they continue to hold this lofty intellectual position, despite the fact that they so seldom manage to live up to it.

As with most other areas of therapeutic endeavour, *building on* the existing strengths tends to be the most effective way of bringing about desirable change. If risk-reduction work starts from the understanding that a parent wants to protect their child, (rather than insisting that they accept their role as out-

and-out abuser), they are far more likely to be able to accept the necessary strategies and shifts in attitude.

SUBSTANCE ABUSE

It is generally recognised that harmful or unwise behaviour which would not otherwise have occurred may be carried out under the influence of alcohol or other mind-altering drugs. This is not, of course, the same thing as saying that the substance use *caused* the behaviour.

Case Example

A study was conducted one Saturday night in a seaside town investigating the relationship between alcohol and offending. Those detained in police cells in the early hours had their blood/alcohol levels tested, and a significant majority were found to be seriously intoxicated. This clearly suggested that alcohol had been an important cause of their offending.

However, the researchers went on to test other individuals still on the streets of the town, who were not suspected of any criminal activity. When their blood/alcohol levels were tested, an *even higher* proportion were found to be severely intoxicated. Clearly, the alcohol alone was not sufficient to explain why one group had offended and the other had not.

The following questions may provide a basic framework for determining the relative role of the substance use in the behaviour. (For simplicity, alcohol is used as the example here.):

1. Has the behaviour *only* occurred in the presence of alcohol or at other times too?
2. Does it occur on *every* occasion that alcohol is used?
3. If not, what are the other necessary conditions? (eg mood, company, amount consumed)
4. Is there evidence that alcohol is used *in order* to carry out the behaviour? or
5. Is the alcohol used *reckless as to whether* the behaviour follows? ie Has the person good reason to expect that it will? or
6. Is the alcohol used as a *reaction* to the behaviour having occurred?

> **Case Example**
> A woman was charged with numerous indecent assaults on the little girl whom she had been babysitting. The parents recalled that on a number of occasions she had been intoxicated when they arrived home, and the woman herself reported that she had been too drunk to know what she was doing; in fact, could remember very little of her actions. In-depth interviews, however, revealed that the assaults had taken place early in the evening when only very little alcohol had been consumed; afterwards, she would drink in order to reduce guilt and anxiety over what she had done.

For those who genuinely do commit harmful acts only when severely intoxicated, clearly the focus of their responsibility lies in the *decision to use the substance in the first place*. In cases of this kind, risk assessment will first need to address the probability of intoxication occurring, as a necessary condition for the behaviour. (In the same way, assessment of a person who offends only when actively psychotic will concentrate on the likelihood of relapse into illness.) However, in a few cases, it may be that the drive to commit the act will continue after its traditional 'cover' has been removed.

> **Case Example**
> A normally mild-mannered teenager had become aggressive towards his peers on a number of occasions under the influence of amphetamines and alcohol. However, after having been placed on probation and successfully controlled his substance abuse, the violence re-emerged at home towards younger siblings.
> It appeared that he had previously been over-protected by his parents, and was unwilling to return to his previous passive style, which had led to his being dominated: in addition, any sign of assertiveness was discouraged by his parents. He had therefore fallen back on the strategy which had won him some form of recognition among his peers, not needing the disinhibiting effects of drugs and alcohol against less threatening opponents.

Substance misuse is often identified as a far more central causal factor in harmful behaviour than it actually is. Perhaps a last important question to be asked is:

7. *Is it possible that both the substance abuse and the harmful behaviour are the result of a third, common factor?*

In the forensic field, offending is frequently attributed to 'drug/ alcohol-induced psychosis'. Further investigation commonly reveals that the picture is rather more complex. Many individuals' traumatic early lives, for example, render them vulnerable to both mental illness *and* substance abuse. Careful history taking can show that moderate drug or alcohol consumption is often not associated with offending until the development of psychosis, when the individual increases their drug intake or drinking in order to deal with these new and frightening phenomena. The offending then begins, perhaps in response to delusional drive, maybe through the disinhibiting effect of the illness, or in order to fund the greater substance abuse. Again, detailed analysis of the psychological and social mechanisms at work, rather than a simple labelling process, is essential in understanding the factors likely to determine future behaviour.

Key questions about controls include:

- *To what extent do the person's moral values and intellectual understanding mitigate against the behaviour?*
- *How do they override such constraints?*
- *Is lack of empathy an influence?*
- *Does the behaviour fit in with self-image?*
- *How realistic is the individual's recognition of the cost of their actions?*
- *Are distorted attitudes and beliefs significant? In what way?*
- *Is the person generally impulsive, in this or other actions?*
- *Is substance abuse influential?*

SEVEN

INSIGHT INTO PAST OFFENDING

MOST OF us are reluctant to acknowledge how much our behaviour is 'driven' by influences not entirely under our control; we prefer to think of ourselves largely as *choosing* to behave as we do. Those who find themselves repeatedly acting unwisely (eg drinking too much) frequently under-rate the strength of the habit, or the difficulty they would have stopping.

As described elsewhere, the processes which lead to a behaviour pattern developing, and those which maintain it, are complex and powerful. Some of the influential factors are to be found in the environment, some in the individual; and some are a combination of both—in other words, factors that the person *actively seeks out or creates* in their environment. Understanding these sources of influence can be extremely significant as a foundation for future control; it is important to assess the degree to which a person is capable of such understanding, and willing to act on it.

RECOGNITION OF DRIVE

As discussed in previous chapters, many people caught in a pattern of undesirable conduct misjudge the strength of the drive behind it. They may prefer to focus on the *product* of their actions (eg 'I'm not a thief, I just had no other way of getting home'), on the *actions of others* (eg 'I've never been into it myself, but I couldn't leave my brother..'), on *accident* (eg 'Suddenly I realised I was outside the very house..') or on more mysterious quirks of fate (eg 'Someone must have spiked my drink with LSD, because then...').

This sort of distortion can be particularly necessary when self-control is basic to the person's self-image, or when the idea of the

---

Case Example

A young woman with a serious heroin addiction was convicted of drug dealing, and received a 12 month prison sentence. She expected to suffer a long and severe withdrawal from the habit, and was surprised to find that the discomfort and craving began to remit after only a week or so. Within a month, she felt in better shape than for several years, and determined never to become a user again when she returned to her dealing activities. In future she would leave the miseries of addiction to her customers; this interval had given her the perspective necessary to break the habit.

On release, in the same frame of mind, she caught the bus from the prison on the outskirts of the city to her home in the centre. However, as she began to recognise familiar landmarks, she began to experience physical discomfort. As the bus passed through areas where she had looked for heroin, been high on it, bought or sold it, and saw fellow users she knew, she realised that she was developing stomach cramps and feeling clammy and shivering, symptoms of withdrawal that she had not felt for months. Three stops from home, she was planning how to get hold of just a small amount of heroin; a one-off, she told herself, as a home-coming celebration.

---

deviant drive is particularly abhorrent. Someone who is in the habit of having sex with prohibited partners (eg children) may deny any specific attraction towards that category of person, but may choose to believe that their partners/victims are merely temporary substitutes for the 'real thing'. A normally conforming individual who drinks too much may argue that they've never liked the taste of the stuff (and so are not real drinkers); they only use it for dutch courage, or to mix socially, or to sleep.

There is usually a core of truth in such rationalisations; this is one of the reasons that treatment designed to reduce maladaptive behaviour must also encourage *adaptive ways of bringing about the same effects*. At the same time, the original triggers for the behaviour (eg boredom, peer pressure, unusual opportunity, anxiety) have often been superseded by more subtle internal reinforcements and have become habitual; it can be difficult to recognise such a shift fully at the time it happens. A young person who starts shoplifting because of peer pressure, for example, may continue it when their peers have stopped because of the particular needs (excitement, challenge etc) which it satisfies. The individual's argument that the undesirable behaviour is still no more than a means to an end can seriously weaken future attempts at control. It is important for them to identify clearly a realistic line between acceptable and non-acceptable conduct.

ACCEPTANCE OF RISK CYCLE

Whether or not a person recognises the motivational drive(s) behind their behaviour, it is common for them to have inadequate insight into the ways in which their own actions have made the behaviour more likely. Sometimes these are obvious to all but the person themselves, as with the problem drinker who gives up alcohol but triggers regular relapses by continuing to play darts for his local pub team. Some are more insidious, and may be closely related to key features of the original behaviour.

Case Example

A man who had previous convictions for serious sexual offences against children moved in with a new wife and her young family. Social Services had laid down strict guidelines for his conduct within the home, to which the couple agreed. In fact, the man himself went on to impose even more stringent limitations on his contact with the children. Having been told that he could not have unsupervised responsibility for them, for instance, he began to react hysterically if one of the children wandered into the garden when he was there alone, shouting in great distress for his wife. Instructed not to go into their bedrooms, he declared sadly that he would not be able to help his wife redecorate in there while the children were away on holiday, and proceeded to blame himself at length to her for his uselessness. Domestic life eventually became impossible, and his wife had to plead with him not to over-react but just to behave with common sense. Even his social worker tried to reassure him that he was only expected to limit *dangerous* behaviour. He was encouraged not to shy away from the children but to show reasonable care and affection. Within 3 months he had indecently assaulted the youngest child, who had become closest to him.

This man's original offences had occurred in a marriage where he had assumed a highly passive, vulnerable role. His advances to his daughters had not been made in a dominating manner, but with the clear message that to refuse him extra affection would destroy him completely. In the new household, he had again managed to create a victim's position so that others were manoeuvred into pushing him towards risk through fear of hurting him more.

The substance abuse field has been the source of invaluable work in this area, culminating in the *Relapse Prevention* model. This approach identifies 'High Risk Factors' (both personal and environmental) in the build-up to the behaviour, enabling the individual to anticipate and recognise them. They are encouraged to explore the often complex, indirect ways in which they set up situations and develop frames of mind where the behaviour is most likely to occur. These have often occurred without the person's full awareness, so that by the time they realised how close they were to falling into the old trap, it was too late.

One of the most important concepts introduced by the Relapse Prevention approach is that of *Apparently Irrelevant Decisions*.

- **Situation:** Aged 16, you have had a huge row with your current and desirable True Love, and sworn never to speak to them again. (Of course, only *part* of you feels this way; the rest is aching for reconciliation.)
- **Behaviour:** Between ranting at your friends over the unforgivable crimes X has committed and how you can never forgive, you nevertheless manage to walk past the places where X is most likely to be on countless occasions. Each time, it is for a perfectly justifiable reason; an errand for your mother, returning X's albums to a mutual friend ...after all, why should you become a recluse ? Rethinking the 'no contact' vow, you feel compelled to write to X, setting out your position and emphasising sadly how it is all over, in terms that seem bound to provoke a response.
- **Result:** Another encounter, for better or worse.

Apparently Irrelevant Decisions tend to be so well backed up by rational reasons that they are hard for others to criticise. When the person themself has some inkling that a decision may not actually be quite as irrelevant as it appears, their defence of it can be even more vigorous. ('Can't I even have a late drink without it being made into a crime?' 'Are you implying that my offering to do the shopping has some ulterior motive ?' 'So I'm supposed to reject all my friends just because some of them have broken the law once or twice ?') Sometimes, the other person's observation itself can be turned into the necessary trigger, using the classic 'Now look what you've made me do'.

A useful analogy for this aspect of Relapse Prevention is that of the behaviour as a magnet and the person as a tintack. Because of the original drive or the learned habit, the behaviour exerts a powerful attraction, which can be resisted only if the person (a) remembers the danger and (b) stays far enough away from it. While the memory of the punitive consequences remains strong, the tintack avoids any direct movement in the direction of the magnet.

However over time, given a reasonable capacity for self-deception, it thinks of reasons why *circling* the magnet at a safe distance might be a good and harmless idea. A common one is to demonstrate the new-found control ('Now that I've kicked the habit completely, I can start to behave normally again instead of avoiding it; prove **I'm** in control of **it**').

Gradually, the 'innocent' manoeuvres bring the tintack within the magnet's range and, if self-deception continues, past the point where internal (conscious, personal) controls are effective.

Another hazardous way of thinking which often leads to 'relapse' is *inflexible reasoning* which states 'If I stick faithfully to these sensible rules at all times, I will be safe'. This attitude often ignores the fact that *the magnet moves as well.*

Many reformed drinkers sworn to abstinence, for example, have been thrown into turmoil when offered sherry trifle. A sex offender who imposes a rule that they will never approach a child may be completely at a loss as to how to react when a child approaches *them*. The most effective approach to this area of risk reduction is to combine *extremely specific behavioural rules with strong general principles* which can be applied to unexpected situations.

A good basic understanding of Relapse Prevention principles is extremely useful in this area of the risk assessment; the process allows the individual's own unique risk factors, as well as some of the more generally influential ones, to be mapped out in relation to future risk. It need hardly be stated, of course, that this process is designed to *increase the assessed person's insight, as well as that of the assessor*. It is to be hoped that the time has long passed when identification of risk factors was perceived as a way of capturing for posterity, like an incriminating photo, the extent of someone's ignorance and self-deception, and them leaving them to stew in it.

UNDERSTANDING OF VICTIM INFLUENCE

It seems to have been assumed by some professionals in the past that the only acceptable view of victim influence by a perpetrator is 'They had no influence; it was all me'. Any offender who implied that their victim might have played a part in their own victimisation was instantly condemned as shifting responsibility and 'blaming the victim'.

In some cases, such as highly violent assaults on strangers, this may well be true. Most offences against the person, however, occur against a background of some sort of relationship, often a long-term one. Even where the behaviour has been clearly excessive or completely inappropriate in that context, it is almost inconceivable that the victim's influence was irrelevant. As discussed in previous chapters, the person committing the harmful act is likely to over-perceive the victim's active contribution to their own victimisation. This predictable distortion, especially understandable where punishment threatens, should not lead the assessor into equivalent or greater distortion.

In disentangling the relative contributions made by individuals involved in a harmful act, an important distinction needs to be made between INFLUENCE and RESPONSIBILITY. **The responsibility for an act always lies entirely with the person who has committed it. Influence on the act can come from a number of sources, including the victim, and can vary in importance from** *peripheral* **to** *necessary for the act to occur.*

A thorough assessment of the harmful behaviour, therefore, needs to identify as precisely as possible the nature of others' influences and the importance of the part they played. In almost every case, access to victim statements will be a necessary aid to this process, and wherever possible, additional interviews with the victim may add important insights.

It is generally accepted, sometimes to an extreme degree, that a perpetrator will misrepresent the harmful episode in order to reduce or avoid punishment. It is useful to bear in mind that there may well be corresponding pressures on *those who have suffered harm* to portray past events in a simplified, unequivocal way. It is natural for people who have been hurt in a traumatic incident to distance themselves from the causes, and to direct blame at those whom they see as responsible. This polarisation tends to happen less where the injury suffered is extreme and/or highly visible, and is more striking where the effects are less obvious or where there is a risk that the victim could also be blamed. In this attempt to emphasise responsibility, ambiguities and subtleties in any past relationship with the offender may be omitted or reduced in significance, so that accuracy is compromised. It is therefore crucial to create a non-judgemental and exploratory atmosphere (similar to that necessary for the offender), where the victim feels able to acknowledge uncertainty, to analyse rather than minimise apparent contradictions, and to identify as accurately as possible their own role in the antecedents to the harmful behaviour. In this way, a far more thorough understanding can be gained of the perpetrator's motivational drive, controls and methods of operating.

A footnote about the implications for victim support and therapy is probably appropriate here. In the climate where victim influence is often significant, but is denied even as a possibility by professionals, immeasurable harm to the victim can be heaped upon the trauma already experienced.

Case Example

A child who had been repeatedly sexually assaulted by her stepfather was assured by the police and counsellors that she had played no part in the abuse. She, however, knew that this was untrue. Every Sunday morning, it had been her job to take her stepfather's morning tea to him in bed, and the cuddles which were part of this custom would frequently end in indecency by him. While hating the sexual part, the little girl had treasured the special physical intimacy, and would jealously guard this weekly duty against attempts by her siblings to share it.

When told, therefore, that she had played no part in the abuse, she had to choose between agreeing to a lie or telling the adults something which was apparently unacceptable to them. It seemed to her that she would only merit their continued support if she had indeed had no influence; and this served to convince her that she must have been doing a very bad thing. Not until a more realistic and accepting therapeutic atmosphere was provided was she able to explore the difference between her influence and his responsibility, and to separate her own natural need for intimacy from her step-father's abusive and inappropriate actions.

INSIGHT INTO PAST OFFENDING

Because so many assaultative incidents occur within existing relationships, one would predict that both positive and negative feelings towards each other will continue to trouble both parties. In much the same way as a bereaved person may need to acknowledge angry feelings towards the person who has died in order to work through their grief, a victim often needs to accept and understand their continuing love, pity or other positive emotion about the perpetrator as well as anger and pain. Gaining a comprehensive and accurate picture of the various influences in the harmful behaviour is often an essential part of the therapist's role in such a process.

Both this area, and that of POWER DISCREPANCY between victim and perpetrator, are analysed more fully in Chapter 10.

ACKNOWLEDGEMENT OF FUTURE RISK

It is extremely common for those who have acted harmfully in the past to predict, perhaps despite overwhelming indications to the contrary, that they will never do such a thing again. The on-the-ball professional will by this stage be familiar with the probability of recidivism for their client, and will be well placed to spot wishful thinking or blind optimism when they see it. They will also appreciate how understandable it is that the person needs to view their future as brighter, to reassure others of this, and to believe that fear of punishment, new insight or just plain willpower will be sufficient to change a deeply-ingrained pattern.

The risk assessment will already have addressed the client's understanding of the nature and strength of their drive, effectiveness of controls, role of disinhibitors, the risk cycle and influence of external factors (including that of the victim, if relevant). Frequently, a skilled and sensitive assessment carried out in a carefully non-judgemental atmosphere will have brought about the maximum degree of insight of which individual is capable at this time. This can make it relatively easy for some to accept the true extent to which they pose a potential threat in the future, and to which they are willing to take protective measures. At the other end of the scale, a person who has felt from the start of the process despised and under attack is unlikely to have accepted either culpability or the need for change. Some risky individuals will of course take this denying, intransigent stance regardless of the way they are treated; a thoughtful and knowledgeable practice will therefore distinguish between the truly resistant and the merely fearful.

Case Example

Two women with numerous previous convictions for shoplifting were seen for their final assessment interviews. Both were asked what they felt they would need to do in order to avoid future offending.

The first had confessed immediately to her offences, acknowledged all along that the thefts were part of a compulsive drive, but stated that she had 'seen the light' and would never behave in such a way again. She insisted that her life would go on entirely as before, but miraculously free from the need to steal. She welcomed the offer of further support, but appeared to see this more as an opportunity to discuss health worries rather than to address her offending. The other woman had denied throughout that she had deliberately stolen, and indeed maintained that she could not remember many of the thefts; she attributed her actions to 'a sort of dream'. In this session, however, she identified a number of internal and external risk factors which she felt had been powerful influences, and also responded actively to explorations by the therapist into ways in which she could protect herself against them. She asked whether further support would be available, while making it quite clear that she was taking control of her problem herself, and only asking for specific task-related help.

The first woman, while meeting all the accepted criteria for 'insight' (ie, agreeing with the assessor's view of her behaviour) was seen as a far higher risk in terms of future offending. Subsequent developments confirmed this prediction; she re-offended within a month, while the second woman has not been re-convicted 3 years later.

Willingness to help design and adhere to a rigorous behavioural preventative regime is frequently, therefore, more significant in future risk reduction than are self-abasing admissions of guilt alone. Mental health professionals should not, on reflection, be surprised at this finding. In no other area of therapy is an early willingness to denigrate oneself considered a good indicator of capacity for personal change. Personal integrity and pride, no matter how precariously based on distorted perceptions, are generally felt to form a good foundation for psychological growth. Working *from* this core of self-belief, rather than attempting to destroy it, is a basic principle of psychotherapeutic work. Just because offenders' underlying problems may have led to harm towards others, there is little reason to suppose that the basic mechanisms necessary for change are any different. While it is perhaps understandable that professionals appalled by the individual's past actions, and anxious to avoid any further harm, may feel the need to express their disapproval and over-predict risk, excessive punishment and demonising of the perpetrator should never be condoned on the grounds that it is *necessary* for effective risk reduction.

ABSENCE OF INSIGHT

A word here about those who are incapable of full insight because of their intellectual or other limitations. Professionals in the learning difficulties field, for example, have long been aware that a lack of insight may not pose an insuperable obstacle to relapse prevention work. Where adequate understanding (of, say, cost to the victim) cannot be harnessed as an incentive to greater control, emphasising of *external constraints* and *negative consequences* are among those approaches which may be powerful in developing a protective strategy. A person whose moral sense remains minimal can benefit from learning more structured rules and limits for her conduct; someone who cannot remember the whole of his pre-offence build-up may be helped to identify one particular (early) point as a cue for some alternative course of action. The new tactics taught are likely to be based on those which have worked for the person in the past.

The professional will also want to assess genuine motivation to change, as distinct from the wish that things were different.

Key questions about insight include:

- To what extent does the individual recognise the strength and patterns of their drive to behave harmfully?
- What are their attitudes towards responsibility/influence? Are these supported by the evidence?
- Are they prepared to take preventative measures?

MOTIVATIONAL STAGE

How many psychologists does it take to change a light bulb? - Only one, but the light bulb's really got to want to change.

Psychologists have traditionally been accused of only being prepared to work with those people who are so insightful, motivated and articulate that they'd probably have been able to change on their own anyway. Like most professional jibes, this isn't entirely true (we do some of our best work with people suffering from learning difficulties and psychosis, for example) but it's *fairly* true. Many people referred for individual therapy are turned down because they don't think they have a problem, because they don't think they have the same problem as the therapist thinks they have, or because they are doubtful that the therapist can help them and are tactless enough to say so.

In these days of fierce budget pruning, too, it has become necessary for all agencies to be selective about the potential users of their service, and many will fasten on to 'insufficient motivation' as a reason. This is perfectly understandable, if indefensible; if there are only enough resources for half of those who walk through the door to obtain a service, some sort of filter process has to operate. An attempt, however ethically suspect, to identify those 'most likely to benefit' is probably more rational than choosing every second person who turns up, or those wearing green. Nonetheless, selection on the basis of an only partially understood concept such as motivation, using idiosyncratic means of measurement, is clearly not ideal. (It may well be argued, for example, that seriousness of the behaviour or likelihood of repeating it, may be more valid criteria.) Where risk assessment is concerned, with the potential for high costs all round whatever the outcome, a more systematic approach is certainly called for.

We sometimes seem to look for motivation as if it were the small area of charted territory on a map of the human psyche, surrounded by the featureless murky wastes of non-motivation marked 'Here be Dragons'! Like 'insight', motivation is often treated as though it were a one-dimensional quality; certainly the *absence* of it tends to be seen in this over-simplified way. However, rejecting an unmotivated person as necessarily beyond immediate help is as foolish as rejecting a motivated one on the grounds that they can do the job themselves *without* help. It is not an simple enough-or-not-enough issue. In the landscape of non-motivation there are many degrees, features and types of obstacle to change; each with its own history and meaning. Each no doubt is navigable using the appropriate strategies and routes on to the next stage, *some of which will be within the power of the therapist* to impart at the time of the therapy/intervention.

We all know, although we sometimes forget, that significant change in attitudes and behaviour does not only occur through

The Stages of 'Non-Motivation'

For the sake of simplicity, four stages of 'non-motivation' are identified here, along with some of the more common factors which can impede progress to the next stage.

Motivational Stage	Blocks to Behaviour Change Include
STAGE M -4 No recognition that there is a a problem, or that viable alternatives exist: includes those who pay only lip-service to need for change	- Lack of knowledge /experience - Threat to self-image - Role models also deviant - Behaviour central to image of self /subcultural group - Fear of greater punishment
STAGE M -3 Recognition of alternatives, but denial of their relevance/desirability for self	- Fear of loss of control - Lack of self-awareness - Congruence of behaviour with other beliefs - Behaviour overshadows other problems
STAGE M -2 Acceptance of relevant and desirable alternatives but unable to envisage change	- Fear of loss of dependency on significant other - Low self-confidence - Threat of changing self-image - Risk of re-interpreting past in new light
STAGE M -1 Minor behaviour change desired in relevant direction	- Limited problem-solving skills - Ignorance of effective strategies - Low self-efficacy - Doubt about worth of minor change

professional intervention. Every individual is on their own unique journey of maturation, with no doubt a top speed for each burst of progress, necessary resting stages and presumably a maximum potential overall. Along the way, their journey can be accelerated, impeded or blocked altogether by experiences they encounter; usually naturally occurring life events, and occasionally deliberate therapeutic efforts. However well-judged and timely such efforts may be, they can only *supplement* the individual's own ability, and must first adjust to that unique pace rather than attempt to override it.

In assessing the individual's ability to reduce future risk, therefore, it is important to recognise:

1. at which motivational stage they are currently functioning,
2. what is obstructing their progress, *and*
3. how ready they are to move on.

Unless the professional has the necessary knowledge and skill to make this evaluation, conclusions such as 'Unmotivated', 'Resistant', 'In denial' or 'Untreatable' can simply mean 'I don't know what it would take for this person to change'.

Having arrived at a comprehensive formulation of the harmful behaviour, the assessing professional will already be in an excellent position to hypothesise about the relevant block(s) in an individual case. Further exploration along the lines suggested above may provide an increasingly detailed picture.

As emphasised earlier, the 'snapshot' function of an assessment, identifying the current state of affairs, now needs to be supplemented by the 'dynamic' indicators. The next step will be to observe or introduce some minimal opportunity for change, in the most favourable circumstances possible, and measure the assessed person's ability to take advantage of this. (If the circumstances of the assessment are necessarily too constraining, or the individual too anxious to benefit from such an exercise, this should of course be reported, and further work in a different setting or at another point in the case recommended. A common example is the period immediately before a court hearing, where efforts cannot be seen as representative of normal motivation.)

The following table suggests some of the approaches and techniques known to be most effective in work with the stages and blocks outlined above.

Aims of Intervention	Techniques May Include
STAGE M - 4	
- To establish neutrality of subject	- Learning from client
- To promote 'objective analytical' approach	- Modelling by assessor and/or others
- To increase information and experience of own and others' behaviour and attitudes	- Information gathering - Information provision
STAGE M - 3	
- To provide non-threatening environment where client can begin to make comparisons and conceptualise alternatives	- As above, *and* - Self-monitoring - Positive feedback - Modelling
- Identification of key drive	- Explore positive consequences
STAGE M - 2	
- Introduce problem-solving approach	- As above, *and* - Explore negative consequences in basic functional analysis
- Identify small, easily-attainable non-threatening goals which will encourage further change	- Access and address key cognitions
- Reinforce self-efficacy	- Identify relevant strengths and achievements - Provide goal breakdown
Stage M - 1	
- Move towards standard methods of behavioural/attitudinal change within Relapse Prevention framework if relevant	- As above, *and* - Identification of High Risk Factors, alternative strategies - Shaping
- Continued emphasis on those techniques already shown to be effective for this person	- Goal setting - Use of punishment (self-imposed)
- Maintain self-determination	- Naturalise reinforcement

It has already been emphasised that the circumstances surrounding risk assessment almost invariably restrict its usefulness as a means of directly obtaining accurate information. Like the police interview, it is a situation which invites, even demands, maximum self-protection by the interviewee. No-one with an average grasp of reality is likely to portray themselves deliberately as risky and unmotivated to change.

As with the other areas of assessment, therefore, indicators of the person's motivational stage and capacity to benefit from intervention will need to be gained from other sources. A car thief who describes vividly to you the trance-like state in which she steals against her will, may well have confided to her hostel manager far less mysterious processes which drive her behaviour. The battered wife is often able to give insight into the tenuous links between her abuser's family patterns and his violence, of which he is well aware but chooses to portray quite differently in your office. Residential staff at a client's old school might be in a better position to estimate his ability to learn from experience, and the approaches which have worked best and worst in the past. In particular, other professionals can often shed light on that perennial problem; differentiation between superficial *consent* and genuine *commitment* to effective intervention.

Key questions about motivation to change include:

- *What stage is the individual currently at?*
- *What appear to be the obstacles to change?*
* *What are the strategies most likely to overcome these?*
- *How useful have these been in the past?*
- *Which approaches have not yet been tried?*

EIGHT

COST OF THE BEHAVIOUR

COST TO THE POTENTIAL VICTIM(S)

WHO IS/ARE the probable victim(s), should the harmful behaviour recur ? A thorough risk assessment should always identify the most likely targets (where there is any indication of this in past acts) in the same way as it defines the type of behaviour being predicted. This may identify:

1. **an individual** ('The risk in question is that of angry sexual violence towards Judy, his wife'),
2, **a specific group of people** ('...deliberate arson endangering the fellow residents of the group home'),
3. **a category of person** ('...serious assault on a male police officer who approaches him for any reason when he has been drinking'),
4. **a risk defined solely by a situation** rather than the identity of the victim ('...threatening behaviour, including verbal abuse and the destruction of property, towards any member of the public who attracts her hostility while she is actively psychotic').

[There are various ways of describing levels of cost, as there are for degrees of probability. For both I prefer High, *Significant* and Low. 'Medium' and 'Moderate' sound to me like settings on a cooker, and in the context of cost to a victim seem rather to understate the intended meaning.]

The cost of a behaviour is normally defined as *High* when it causes severe suffering and/or damage to the victim, and particularly when these effects are irreversible. *Low* cost

81

behaviours, while causing some damage, injury or distress, are those considered in general to be tolerable within stated limits (see *Applied Cost* Chapter 10). *Significant* cost spans the area between; behaviour neither tolerable nor probably irreversible.

The reaction of the victim is clearly an important indicator of cost. Indeed, a recent judicial proclamation suggests that this can be taken into account when sentencing an offender. This can clearly give rise to a distorted application of justice, however. In some cases, the 'injured party' may report being able to tolerate the behaviour, even welcoming or instigating it, while the law or social norms define it as harmful. Another victim may describe the experience as intensely distressing and beyond their control, while the circumstances of the incident and independent accounts suggest otherwise, or indicate that for most people (ie other potential victims), the cost would be lower. Nevertheless, in the majority of (non-fatal) cases, the victim's reaction often influences the public view of the cost of the behaviour to a significant degree.

When child sexual abuse was still a relatively new area, (academically and clinically that is), it used to be implied by some professionals that the cost of *any* inappropriate sexual behaviour towards a child was by definition unacceptably high. As more detailed information has become available about the prevalence and effect of this type of experience in people's lives, however, it has become possible to develop more sophisticated and sensitive ways of assessing cost to victims. It is no longer considered some sort of obscene heresy to suggest, on the basis of careful assessment, that the cost of a further incident of abuse may in fact be tolerable under certain conditions, or preferable to another state of affairs such as the disintegration of a family. Influential work such as that by David Finkelhor and Angela Browne has begun to identify some of the individual components of sexual abuse believed to be related to its harmful effects, such as *betrayal by trusted figures, age-inappropriateness* and *invasiveness* of the abuse, *blurring of responsibility* for the events, and the *response of others* to the child's reports of what has happened. Other research has identified *previous family dysfunction* as an important influence on the degree of harm resulting from the later abuse. Such indirectly-related factors are also important in determining cost to the individual, because they can sometimes clarify the issue of *intended* or *foreseeable cost*, compared to that actually caused (see *Applied Cost* Chapter 10).

Case Example

A. A driver parks his brand new Jaguar on a hill, unaware that the handbrake is faulty. It rolls down the hill and into a river.

B. The same scenario, but this time the car rolls down the hill into a crowd of school children at a bus stop causing serious injury.

Which of the drivers is more to blame? Is the one whose car causes greater harm guilty of greater negligence? The issue of *intent* or *preventable harm* is clearly also an issue.

One further issue for consideration is that of *escalation*.

The first question to ask is whether a trend towards greater cost to victims is already discernable in the behaviour pattern of the individual. The second is whether the past actions demonstrate any of the recognised *indicators of escalation*. A recent study of indecent exposers, for example, has confirmed clinical observations that the majority of these offenders continue to behave in much the same way throughout their careers: roughly 25%, however, appear to go on to commit contact sexual offences. The research has identified a number of factors associated with the early offending of that escalating minority. While these and similar indicators cannot have 100% predictive accuracy (ie some of those who display the 'risk factors' will not escalate, and some who go on to offend more seriously will have presented none of them), they should be referred to, *along with the reported significance levels*. For example, research could show that the presence of certain 'escalation indicators' could increase the probability of a serious future assault from 10% to 25% (but still less likely to happen than not), or from 10% to 80% (more likely than not); this distinction needs to be made clear in a responsible assessment.

COST TO THE PERPETRATOR

While this issue does not, strictly speaking, fall into the formal risk assessment framework, it certainly needs to be taken into account overall.

In some cases, the cost of *over-prediction* could mean a catastrophic loss for the person being assessed. Long-term separation from partner and family, continued detention or compulsory psychiatric treatment may result from being labelled 'High Risk'. While this does not mean that obvious riskiness should ever be ignored or understated, it should alert the professional to address even more thoroughly any possible sources of error, and to identify ways in which *capacity to change* may be assessed further, now and in the longer term.

For other assessed individuals, the costs of *under-prediction* are the more critical, because the person cannot afford to fail. A psychiatric in-patient who has found it extremely difficult to adjust to a succession of hostel placements may be offered what is in effect a 'last chance', so that premature or insufficiently supported rehabilitation could be extremely damaging. A convicted offender serving a suspended sentence or probation order following a serious offence has more to lose from even a minor misdemeanour, and thus from an inadequate appreciation of the risk factors in re-offending.

While it is clearly not acceptable to doctor the conclusions of a well-conducted assessment to fit the circumstances of the assessed person, it *is*, however, particularly important to specify all the possible influences and how they can be best managed in order to reduce risk. A graded programme (eg of rehabilitation, exposure to the victim) might be drawn up, with decreasing degrees of supervision recommended as skills develop and potential risk factors are explored and addressed. Such a programme maximises the likelihood that identified warning signs will be recognised at an early stage and that small problems can be dealt with (and the process halted if necessary) before they become unmanageable.

COST TO ASSESSOR (AND THE SERVICE)

Practitioners have a responsibility to protect themselves and their employing organisations, in parallel with their obligations to the client and to potential victims (ie society). While this is rarely acknowledged openly, self-protection is nevertheless a powerful influence on decisions about risk.

Imagine that the national news has recently focused on an incident in which a depressed person discharged from a psychiatric hospital has killed their family and then themselves in gruesome circumstances, or where a child on the At Risk Register is found to be severely physically abused for the second time. It would be naive to believe that around the country, fellow professionals do not make (or carefully consider making) rather more cautious decisions in the short term about similar cases on their own caseloads. In other types of decisions, longer-term public attitudes about certain client groups mean that systematically more cautious or risky decisions tend to be made *way beyond the demands of the case itself and the needs of the individuals concerned,* because of the greater punishment for error attached to the decision.

It is clearly not desirable for professional actions to be motivated primarily by fear of negative consequences; where this consistently outweighs the positive drive to do a good job, there is likely to be a marked deterioration in quality of practice. It is certainly a fact of life, however, that if we are to be allowed to continue to carry out this difficult and essential work, we need to retain some degree of public confidence. In particularly sensitive cases, therefore, decisions are invariably made not only on the basis of risk of harm to the client or the public, but also in order to maintain the reputation of the institution.

Case Example

An elderly disabled man who had spent many years in a Special Hospital following serious arson offences was about to be discharged back to his home area. He enjoyed a drink, and on his first two unescorted trips outside the hospital had over-indulged himself at the nearby pub and wobbled back happily but erratically in his wheelchair, to the amused concern of passers-by.

The clinical team responsible for his care were aware that alcohol was not implicated in his past offending, and that he was at no great risk of harm to himself through this practice during the few weeks before his discharge. They were also sensitive to his rehabilitation needs prior to his return to the community. Their decision to withdraw his unescorted leave, and to provide a supervising nurse on subsequent trips, was made on the basis that he was breaking the hospital limits for alcohol consumption, and could jeopardise the delicate relationship that the hospital had with local residents. The balance between security and therapy was achieved, the team felt, by adding an alcohol education component to the patient's programme which helped to structure the supervised trips.

In this case, the hospital staff were aware that their ban on unlimited drinking would only apply until his discharge,

---

and chose instead to use *escorted* pub trips as the least restrictive but still manageable option. Had the above incident occurred in a long-stay residential home, on the other hand, an unlimited restriction on the man's freedom of movement and choice of leisure activity would probably, and rightly, have been considered unethical.

Risk decisions involve duty to the client, duty to society and to the organisation; the relative costs and benefits to all three therefore need to be taken into account before they can be prioritised in the prevailing situation. A serious distortion can occur where the professionals believe that 'duty to the organisation' is an unacceptable consideration in decision making and deny that it influences them. Fear of getting it wrong persists, however, and in order to justify their actions they may convince themselves that either the probability of harm is greater, or the cost to the victim higher, than it really is.

Key questions about the cost of the behaviour include:

- *Who is / are the most likely victim / s?*
- *Is low, significant or high cost indicated?*
    - *to the victim?*
    - *to the perpetrator?*
    - *to the professionals involved?*

SECTION THREE

FACTORS IN APPLIED RISK: THE INFLUENCE OF A KNOWN ENVIRONMENT ON HARMFUL BEHAVIOUR

The last section outlined those aspects of the *person* which contribute to their future behaviour; the risk represented by the individual in their stockinged feet, as it were.

An assessment which has progressed this far will have addressed the *potential* of the individual to behave in a certain way. It is now necessary to identify the influence of external factors on that potential; will the probability of such behaviour be increased or reduced by the environment in which the person is likely to find themselves ?

Behind many requests for risk assessment lies a concern about a specific setting and identified victim/s. 'Is Ms X safe to return to her children ?' 'How likely is a recurrence of firesetting by Mr B if placed in a hostel as opposed to a flat of his own ?' 'Will the risk of harm to this baby be increased if his parents live together rather than apart ?' In others, (for example some prison parole reports), an assessment of risk may be required without clear details being provided as to the future environment. In such cases, it should be made clear by the assessor that any prediction will invariably be weakened by the lack of this important information.

The chapters in this section look at significant aspects of the environment in which the behaviour may occur, suggest the range of factors which can influence the individual's capacity to cause harm and consider the professional's ability to detect it sufficiently early.

NINE

EMOTIONAL/SOCIAL ENVIRONMENT

FUNDAMENTAL QUESTIONS to be asked at this stage will include:

- *What are the significant emotional and social characteristics of the environment/s in which this behaviour has occurred before?*
- *How similar are these factors to those which they are likely to be encountered in the future?*
- *Has the individual acted harmfully in a wide range of situations, or only in very specific ones?*
- *Who were the significant others involved, and what was their influence?*

SIGNIFICANT OTHERS: INTIMATE RELATIONSHIP FACTORS

For most of us, the quality of our close relationships exerts a powerful influence over our emotional well-being and capacity to maintain control over our lives. In general, it seems reasonable to argue that when we feel loved and valued, our personal and professional standards are more easily maintained, we feel more highly motivated to work for long-term goals, and have greater control over self-indulgent or destructive habits.

But is that actually true? No doubt everyone can bring to mind a good friend or relative who, having fallen for someone they thought the world of, began to develop a lifestyle or pattern of behaviour which to others seemed quite undesirable. Apart from the fact that they have less time for you (unwelcome enough in itself), friends who are half of a couple often seem to compromise too much, relinquish some of their more worthy and interesting traits, get sloppy about things you valued in them, develop unattractive weaknesses. (Incredibly, the same accusations might be levelled at you in similar circumstances!) At another level, all practitioners can certainly bring to mind patients/ clients whose episodes of instability were directly attributable to the influence of their nearest and dearest:

> *It would be a dangerous over-simplification to suggest that social isolation or loss of a valued relationship are necessary or sufficient to increase riskiness, and that stable relationships are bound to reduce such risk.*

An essential starting point for this part of the assessment, therefore, is to understand the particular ways in which the person in question has responded to significant others in the past.

Case Example

A young man who had committed numerous indecent exposures was asked by a psychologist about the state of his sexual relationship since his marriage 2 years previously. He reported considerable frustration that intercourse did not happen as frequently as he would wish; his wife, on the other hand, reported that in fact she was the one who made more sexual demands. The psychologist in her report concluded that the husband was probably giving the more accurate account. This was assumed on the basis that his sexual frustration more closely 'fitted' the psychologist's theories about this type of offence.

While frustration is indeed a significant factor for many indecent exposers, however, it transpired that the opposite was true for this individual. Never having experienced a long-term sexual relationship before, he had previously had no difficulty in maintaining a virile and almost predatory self-image. However, when faced with his wife's eagerness, his belief in his own sexual dominance became increasingly threatened, and for the first time in his life he began to suffer from impotence. The indecent exposure allowed him to regain the sense of being an unpredictable sexual force to be reckoned with, rather than a regular supplier who could not always meet the demand.

In this case, therefore, adequate sexual gratification within a stable relationship actually *increased* the risk of his offending.

The emotional needs of an individual may be such that they almost invariably choose partners who are unable to meet them. Sometimes childhood experiences drive them to seek a partner similar to an unsatisfactory parent, in the subconscious hope that they might make it work differently this time (eg by being more worthy, or tougher, or more desirable). Many instinctively choose those who are as needy as themselves and equally lacking in nurturing ability, so that mutual disappointment and recrimination are inevitable. Others seem to drive quite adequate partners into the positions they most fear.

Any of these types of unsatisfactory intimate arrangements can increase harmful behaviour in some individuals, through distress, anger and hopelessness. In others, domestic unhappiness may be completely unrelated to the behaviour, or might actually reduce it. Domination by a parent or partner, for example, to a degree that most would consider excessive and unhealthy, will have very different effects on the subordinate individuals involved.

Case Example

In my own out-patient clinic in a small county town, two young men from the same remote village demonstrated contrasting responses to their similarly repressive family backgrounds. One, mercilessly bullied for years by his Spiritualist father, developed a 'psychic ability' to transmit messages from beyond the grave, some of which directed him regularly to send obscene anonymous letters to respectable local ladies. It was certainly the only way he could have expressed any angry or sexual feelings without severe punishment from his father, and was likely to continue at least as long as normal avenues were closed to him.

The other lad had led a similarly restricted life with his over-controlling grandmother, but remained wholly law-abiding (though resentful) until her death, when he developed a habit of compulsive voyeurism. After a series of court appearances and countless failed attempts at intervention, he began to cohabit with an extremely forceful and aggressive young woman who, to all appearances, made his life a misery. The offending came to an abrupt halt, no doubt through the re-imposition of the firm external structure which was by now a necessary substitute for his impoverished internal controls.

In many cases, particularly those involving teenage and young adult offenders, relationship difficulties lie at the root of the deviant behaviour. Some relationships may be so disturbed that they seem sufficient to explain the offending, or it may be the special vulnerability of the individual which renders them unable to cope with those particular dynamics.

Despite the frequency with which professionals identify relationships as key causal factors, there is an astounding lack of appropriate provision to address these difficulties. Mental health practitioners routinely offer individual therapy even when it is clear that some 'significant other' is central to the problem. It must be similarly evident to many agencies who provide 'offending behaviour' programmes that such systems are often dealing with symptoms rather than causes. Involving partners and families in addressing fundamental relationship issues is therefore an crucial part of both assessment and intervention in managing risk.

Case Example

A young man whose violent behaviour had escalated over recent months referred himself for help through his GP. He reported an alarming lack of concern for his victims and a deep sense of pride in vanquishing them, but confessed that he was worried about the possibility of attracting a prison sentence were he to be arrested again.

Previous assessments had focused on the high tolerance for violence in his notoriously hostile neighbourhood and peer group, suggesting that he was largely a product of this setting. However, it was clear this time that he had exceeded even these extreme limits, and his fear of incarceration provided the clue to the most significant influence in his life. His father had left home before he was born, and he had taken on the role of 'man of the house' early in his childhood. His mother had apparently encouraged any sign of aggressive machismo, and still proudly paraded him around the town when he accompanied her on shopping trips, much as one might show off a huge and bristling guard dog.

Although she too had become concerned about his increasingly out-of-control violence and its possible consequences, she had been unable to help him distinguish between acceptable and unacceptable aggression. Meanwhile, he continued to believe that to modify his angry reactions to others would be to betray his role as family Dobermann.

After individual interviews with both mother and son, a joint session was arranged. She was encouraged to give a clear message to her son about the robust belligerence she valued in him, in contrast to the vindictive attacks which she felt put him and the family at risk. For the first time he began to perceive how self-restraint could be compatible with his role within the family.

Key questions in assessing the influence of intimate relationships in an individual's behaviour will include:

- *What does the individual appear to need from an intimate relationship?*
- *Do they seem able to choose the sort of person who can provide this consistently?*
- *How does it effect them when their emotional needs are met / unmet? Has this been linked to their harmful behaviour / offending in the past?*
- *How likely is it that those closest to them will be able to relate to them in such a way that the harmful behaviour is less likely?*

SIGNIFICANT OTHERS: SUB-CULTURAL INFLUENCES

A sub-culture is a group within a group; for our purposes an identifiable sector of society with beliefs, values, codes of conduct, and sources of reinforcement and punishment which differ from those of the wider culture. The sub-cultural group which exerts an influence on an individual's riskiness may be as small as a nuclear family group, as large as a nation, or something in between (eg bikers, residents of a neighbourhood, Hunt Saboteurs).

As mentioned earlier in this chapter, the assumption that social integration leads to greater emotional and behavioural stability is an over-simplification. Some recent work with people discharged from psychiatric hospital, for example, found that many individuals rated as more socially isolated were actually *less* at risk than their more sociable counterparts. They were not so likely to run into difficulties nor to be re-admitted to hospital within the follow-up period than were those who operated within a social network. It is probable that the *type* of social group (as well as the sub-culture of which it is part) is a critical factor behind these findings.

The most obvious examples of *risk-enhancing* groups are those which advocate or encourage risk-taking behaviour, from the illegal to the merely hedonistic or undisciplined. Sub-cultures in which substance abuse is valued, for example, are likely to increase the problem of inadequate controls for some individuals, while those which require their members to prove themselves through rule violation or aggression will be a particular danger to other vulnerable types.

Clearly, though, not all members of such groups commit harmful acts, despite the prevailing anti-social attitudes or stimulation-seeking activities. Those who do so are often people with few appropriate role models, relatively weak self-esteem or a fragile sense of personal identity, such that they depend more heavily on identification with the group. Sometimes their peers are well aware of their greater need for approval, and will goad them on to excesses at which the more stable group members would draw the line (or which they would certainly carry out more successfully). In other cases, the sub-culture may actually be unaware of the adherence of the weaker individual:

Case Example

One young woman referred by the courts had a history of repeated but unrelated vendetta against those she saw as perpetrators of injustice. Drawn to any situation in which she believed a blameless victim to be badly treated, she would become intensely committed to vengeance, usually with the victim's cooperation, but sometimes to their acute discomfort. Because of her fear of outright confrontation, her campaigns would usually involve passive-aggressive tactics such as threatening telephone calls, vandalism and nuisance hoaxes.

Her supervising Mental Health Team encouraged her ambition to try volunteer work at the local RSPCA kennels, hoping that this opportunity for *positive* response to neediness would act as a substitute for the negative behaviour of the past. Without their knowledge, however, she applied to become an RSPCA Inspector: rejected as unsuitable, she used the organisation's records to identify suspected cruelty cases, and began another series of revenge attacks on the people concerned. When re-arrested, she was found to have built up a collection of radical animal liberation-style literature, and had clearly modelled her actions on her own interpretation of their aims and methods.

> As in the previous offences, she had avoided formal group
> membership, through a reluctance to be restricted by the
> teamwork ethos and discipline that this would involve.

There are many other examples of risk being increased
through *personal identification at a distance* rather than direct
social contact with others. Adoption of role models from films and
TV is an common enough phenomenon: despite widespread
concern about the effects of screen violence, most people are able
to distinguish between behaviour it is safe to copy and extreme
acts which are impressive but obviously inappropriate to
everyday life. The vulnerable few, however, go further than
admiring the behaviour or envying its fictional payoff. They can
become preoccupied with the portrayal of the character, over-
identify with his or her perceived feelings and motives, and re-
enact in imagination their own version of the key scenes until
they believe that they too are capable of the behaviour.

Similar reactions occur in the aftermath of horrific and well-
publicised crimes. It is not uncommon for inadequate and
disturbed individuals to unnerve their therapists and other
professionals by claiming parallels with serial killers and
notorious sadists. Fortunately, most of them derive enough gain
from such identification and fantasy that they are able to stop
short of acting it out (if indeed this was ever the intention).
Others will report a repugnance for the crimes they have heard
about, but an overwhelming fear that they will somehow feel
compelled to do something similar; this tends to be anxiety-
related rather than the result of a deviant drive. (It should never
be assumed, of course, that such concerns or threats are merely
hollow gestures; of the few who do go on to carry out their
harmful fantasies, a number will have expressed their intentions
beforehand. A full assessment as outlined in Section 2 is still
indicated, therefore, unless there are weighty reasons against it.)

Finally, some subcultural influences seem to affect the
vulnerable individual in a paradoxical way, the group in question
being clearly unexceptional in its own values and behaviour.
Examples of this would be the person who regularly becomes
assaultative in respite care, or whose self-injurious behaviour
tends to follow attendance at a low-key day centre. I think of this
as the 'Vicarage Tea Party Phenomenon'. We are all aware of
times when, surrounded by extremely well-behaved people, or in
an over-regulated setting, we are seized by a dreadful and

glorious urge to behave appallingly, to render ourselves utterly unacceptable to them all. At a less frivolous level, a similar reaction can occur in situations where the conventional mode of communication seems inadequate to express our needs (for example, when in hospital and in great pain or discomfort). In these situations, the orderly and controlled atmosphere, in fact the very discipline which underpins the value of the place, can provoke the distressed individual to extreme behaviour which feels consistent with their own, isolated, experience.

In training for professionals on de-escalation of aggressive face-to-face encounters, 'mood-matching' is an essential component. This technique involves the professional presenting an equivalent level of arousal to that expressed by the client/ patient, while also modelling control and a determination to solve the problem constructively. Clearly, similar mood-matching must also occur in groups with which the individual is expected to identify. If a very agitated person finds themselves among those who are much more ordered and calm, they may well feel alienated and panicky, and seek to *emphasise* the gulf which they feel powerless to bridge. While it is a sound principle that to progress, a person needs role models who have already achieved some of the same goals, it is vital that the discrepancy between achiever and non-achiever is not too great, or it will almost invariably prove counter-productive.

Key questions about subcultural influences include:

- *Who are the people / figures whose example or approval are most important to the individual?*
- *Do these significant others require, encourage or demonstrate harmful behaviour?*
- *Do they indulge in behaviour which, while relatively safe for them, is potentially harmful or disinhibiting for the individual in question?*
- *Does the individual tend to behave in an extreme or risky way as a result of contact with these other people, despite the group's more conventional / stable behaviour?*

SITUATIONAL TRIGGERS

In many cases, it will be the *characteristics of the situation* in which the individual finds themselves, rather than the specific behaviour of other people, which will serve as triggers for the key behaviour.

'Ambient' factors

Sometimes, it is the emotional climate, general atmosphere or longer-term demands which render the individual vulnerable. Material deprivation, absence of status, powerlessness and uncertainty, for example, are among the situationally-related factors which are commonly associated with increased risk. Some people react poorly to extra autonomy, others to a lack of it. What constitutes a nicely stimulating lifestyle to one will be experienced as intolerably dull to another. A financially cautious person can become seriously anxious when they have to break into their nest-egg, while someone else lives on a spectacular overdraft without concern. As in so many other areas of the assessment, therefore, it is the *individual's reaction in the past* to their long-term conditions which is significant, not the apparent abnormality of the conditions nor the extent to which they would unsettle the average person.

Some of the ambient factors may be clearly linked to the behaviour in that they raise the vulnerable individual's level of awareness or opportunity. A home in which nudity is commonplace, or sleeping arrangements unusual, for example, may increase the likelihood of inappropriate sexual conduct in a person with inadequate controls. A family ethos of rule violation or risk-taking may be sufficient to encourage anti-social acts in someone impressionable. Again, the atmosphere need not in itself be exceptional or deviant for its effect on the individual to be damaging in terms of their own riskiness.

Precipitating factors

Some behaviours are the result of an underlying vulnerability in combination with a triggering stimulus, rather than (or as well as) a background atmosphere. An important loss, or the fear of one; a threat to personal control, a perceived insult to self or another, a disappointment, an invasion or frustration of a drive may all precipitate a re-emergence of the behaviour in question.

In a series of harmful actions, the key factor linking the antecedent events may be less than obvious. A fight over the wrong change in a fish and chip shop, walking out of a new job and kicking the lawnmower to pieces are fairly disparate at first glance: the common precipitant could turn out to be a powerful sense of being humiliated and made to feel stupid. Sometimes the trigger and the behaviour are widely separated in time or space (eg being thwarted at work, then hitting a traffic warden 2 days later), which can obscure the causal link. Careful functional analysis may be needed to draw out the common denominator/s.

Key questions about the significant situational characteristics include:

- *What factors have been common to situations in which this behaviour has occurred before?*
- *To what degree have these factors needed to be present for the behaviour to occur? (eg minor or severe loss, real or anticipated threat, extreme or slight provocation).*
- *How likely is it that these factors will occur again in the individual's current / proposed environment?*

TEN

VICTIM FACTORS

THIS CHAPTER deals with predictions about the risk of harm to one or more other people. While the majority of risk assessments fall into this category, the most common exceptions involve harm to the individual themselves and to property.

Even where the harm is likely to be self-inflicted, it is useful to consider for a moment whether *indirect* harm to others is also a possibility. How scrupulous, for example, is the arsonist in checking that no-one is in danger from the fires she sets in (apparently) empty buildings? What would it take for the person attempting suicide to kill a member of their family first, or to enter into a pact with someone else? If a bystander unexpectedly intervened in a future robbery, what is the likelihood that the robber would react violently? Even if the possibility seems remote, it may still be worth mentioning, along with a clear statement about the strength or weakness of relevant indicators.

INFLUENCE AND RESPONSIBILITY

The responsibility *for an act always lies exclusively with the person who commits it.*

The influences *on the act may arise from a variety of sources, including the victim, and can be of different degrees of importance.*

We have no difficulty in accepting this proposition when it is applied to everyday interpersonal behaviour. Take rudeness from shop assistants, for example. If you approach them with 'Two of those and hurry up about it', you may not be surprised if they are less than friendly in response (although some still manage to be incredibly courteous in the face of this sort of treatment). Others may foil all your attempts to be pleasant, and display a vigorous insolence regardless. We recognise that some people will almost always behave rudely, that others rarely do, and that most respond to the way that they themselves are treated, their behaviour being more sensitive to influence by others. When considering offending behaviour, where the consequences to the victim are usually much greater, this vital distinction between responsibility and influence is often overlooked.

As discussed in Chapter 5, the strength of the internal drive to commit a harmful act may vary considerably between one individual and another.

100% Internally Driven	100% Externally Driven

In other words, some behaviour is the result of such a powerful drive that it will occur regardless of the setting, some will happen only in the most extreme circumstances, and most falls somewhere in between.

Where the internal drive is strong enough, victim influence is unlikely to make much difference. The great majority of injurious behaviours *are* influenced by others, however, and it is important to evaluate how much, and in what way.

Case Example

In cases of sexual assault on children, perpetrators will often describe their victims as sexually knowing, experienced or provocative. This has become viewed as such an unacceptable statement from an offender that it is almost automatically assumed to be untrue and culpable. I once attended a Child Protection Case Conference in which such an offender attempted to describe how, having moved in with his girlfriend, he had allowed himself to respond to the sexually provocative behaviour of her 12 year old daughter. He knew he was entirely to blame for doing so, he said, but he just wanted to explain to the Conference how it had been.

He withdrew from the meeting, at which point his statement was unanimously condemned as 'highly alarming ... clear evidence of denial ... projection of guilt'. Shortly after, reports from the child's head teacher described exactly that same behaviour *pre-dating* the offender's presence in the household. Everyone nodded sagely. No-one seemed to think that their reactions to the two reports were at all inconsistent. In fact, when the similarities between the two descriptions of the child were pointed out, several people became quite incensed, suggesting that this observation was 'collusive'.

The agitation appeared to be created by that basic confusion between influence and responsibility, and the suspicion that to identify the significant role of the victim was to imply that she *caused* or *justified* what happened to her.

When a householder seriously injures an intruder in defence of his home and family, the influence of the thief is absolutely *necessary* for his assault to occur. At the other end of the scale, a paedophile cruising school playgrounds might pick one child rather than another because of her individual appearance and mannerisms: he may well be determined to assault anyway, but her influence merely *directs* his behaviour. A mother with anger control problems may beat her baby because of his refusal to feed; here his age-appropriate responses are sufficient to *trigger* violent behaviour to which his mother was predisposed.

In other cases, of course, the influence may come from someone other than the eventual victim. Insulted and ridiculed by work colleagues, a person might take it out on members of their own family. A child may be abducted by a parent in revenge towards their unfaithful partner. An adolescent whose clumsy advances are rejected may assault the next young woman he judges to be sexually active but unlikely to want him. Sometimes the victim in this sort of situation will also have provided a minor influence (expressing mild criticism, behaving thoughtlessly). They may sometimes be provoked into doing so by the perpetrator, who has already identified them as the appropriate target and needs only a token trigger.

The above examples involve victim influence which is *innocent, appropriate*, or at worst, *merely unwelcome*. In other harmful acts, the influence may in itself be aggressive, reckless or even intended to bring about the behaviour in question.

> **Case Example**
> A married couple attended an out-patient clinic in which the husband was being assessed for treatment of his extreme jealousy of and violence towards his wife. Some way into the interview, both were asked to identify *positive* functions of the violence in their relationship. They found this difficult, as both had agreed that separation would be inevitable if the husband could not learn to control his outbursts completely.
> Finally, after much discussion, his wife commented that, when he hit her for some perceived sign of infidelity, at least she knew he still cared about whether she was faithful or not. He appeared unable to express this is a positive way, such as saying that he loved her, or that he was anxious that she might leave him. In fact, she recalled, occasionally, when he seemed to have become distant or indifferent, she had deliberately behaved in a way which she knew was likely to elicit a jealous reaction, in order to reassure herself of his regard. It was clear that any treatment programme would need to include training for this man in more appropriate emotional expression, and that his wife might also need to be included in part of the work.

Key questions about victim influence include:

- *How unusual was the victim's behaviour, compared to the way that most people would have behaved in that situation?*
- *If the victim's behaviour was unusual, does the historical evidence suggest that the perpetrator's reaction has occurred **only** in the presence of such unusual influence?*
- *How able was the victim to predict that the perpetrator would react in the way they did?*

AVAILABILITY

Perhaps it sounds obvious that there needs to be an available victim in an event which involves harm to another. The important issue to be considered is: *how available does a victim need to be?* As we have already seen, in extreme cases the motivational drive behind the harmful behaviour is so powerful and/or so indiscriminate that a suitable victim will always be found. A compulsive shoplifter living in the city can always find a suitable shop. Someone who invariably becomes assaultative when drunk, and who is determined to carry on drinking to excess, will have no difficulty in running into adequate provocation for their violence. In these examples, there is evidence of a probably deviant drive and of little discrimination between targets.

Alternatively, the common denominator between victims may well indicate *normal drive* combined with *restricted normal opportunity* rather than active deviance or genuine victim preference. An elderly, bedridden male resident of a nursing home who indecently assaults young members of the nursing staff could actually be far more strongly attracted to women of his own age, but nevertheless poses a risk to any non-threatening female within arm's reach. A hospital in-patient with severe learning difficulties may repeatedly abscond to steal from his terrified mother, after planned and supervised visits home have been suspended through staff shortages. In such situations, it will be necessary to identify ways in which *blocked outlets* for a normal drive contribute to the choice of victim.

In general, where the deviant drive is sufficiently strong, or normal opportunities severely limited, significant victim factors tend to be those which might just *reduce* the probability of harm to certain people, rather than those which make it more likely. In the earlier examples given, the shoplifter could be equally drawn to any large local store, with the exception of those in which he has already been arrested and will easily be recognised again. For the elderly nursing-home resident, while age or obvious seniority might render a nurse ineligible for molestation, any other woman would be at high risk whatever her appearance or behaviour. The only selection factors are those which *disqualify* some potential victims.

Where there has been a wide range of victims and offending situations in the past, clearly availability is not such an obstacle to further harm. Here containment of the drive or of the individual themselves will be necessary to reduce future risk.

However, most risky individuals exercise some *selection* (not necessarily consciously) of the targets for their actions. Few rapists, for example, seem completely indiscriminate as to the women they choose; some restrict their attacks to a particular age range, some to females whom they perceive as being promiscuous or demeaning, others to victims who are personally dependent on them in some way. A parent who has severely physically abused all their own offspring may have behaved impeccably towards other children in their care. The violent drinker may have attacked numerous men, but all of them roughly his own age and size, and may never have assaulted a woman or child, despite ample opportunity and equivalent provocation from them.

Case Example

A young man who had indecently exposed himself to numerous teenage girls was asked about his choice of victim. He reported somewhat boastfully that no choice was involved; he merely took up position when he was ready and exposed to the first unaccompanied female who came along. Information from the police officers involved, however, suggested strong similarities between his previous victims. All those who had come forward to report his behaviour had been aged 15-19, short-haired, small in stature, lacking obvious confidence or poise and unobtrusively dressed.

Further interviewing with the young man focused on his reactions on seeing a potential victim approach, and it soon became evident that he was instantly inhibited by what he perceived as sexual confidence or experience. Women who appeared older, larger, more self-assured or more fashionably dressed than himself intimidated him, and he feared their response. He would withdraw into the shadows and wait for someone who looked as if they would be more impressed by him. (Their fearful reaction, incidentally, he neither intended nor wanted; his unrealistic hope was that his victim would see him as a desirable sexual partner.)

Other individuals will be extremely limited in their range of victims, or in the variety of settings within which they will behave harmfully (see Chapter 9). This may be the result of an unexceptional or even low drive, which requires enormous external influence in order to manifest itself in damaging action. It has been argued that the majority of people who kill, for example, would never have done so but for the unique dynamics between themselves and their victim; such people probably represent negligible further risk to others. Similarly, a man who has only average sexual arousal to under-age girls, and normally adequate controls against responding to this arousal, may be susceptible only to *pro-active* attempts at sexual contact by such a child, and even then only within an environment which explicitly emphasises children's sexuality.

Where it appears that some specific characteristic or behaviour of the victim is necessary to trigger the harmful act, it may be useful to explore the possibility that the perpetrator may have in turn been a pro-active influence previously. Some regular offenders set up situations or conversations in which the key trigger by the victim is then more likely to occur.

Case Example

One man convicted of rape described his victim as unacceptably promiscuous, a *sufficient* trigger for him. The victim's statement however told how she had been pestered for some time by his questions about how many boyfriends she had had. These seemed to be made in a joking and admiring way, and she had played along, replying that she had had 'thousands' of sexual encounters. This was the answer he had been looking for, and he chose to deny to himself that he had encouraged her to reply in this way.

Another young man assured me that he had only assaulted a fellow drinker when the man insulted his mother. This seemed fairly reasonable, until he reluctantly admitted to having earlier told a series of anecdotes at her expense, after which the other man agreed with him that she must indeed be an 'old bag'. Ruminating drunkenly on this later in the evening, the young man returned to attack his companion for his uncharitable assessment!

A narrow range of victims may also result from a drive which is strong, but highly specific. A car thief may feel compelled purely to steal a certain make of high-performance vehicle: a sadistic rapist might be sufficiently motivated to inflict suffering only on a partner whom he already dominates emotionally. It is often erroneously supposed that an irresistible deviant drive is inevitably indiscriminate; for example, that someone with a severe drink problem will drink anything they can get their hands on. Not so; one of my alcohol-dependent patients would drink champagne through choice and after-shave through necessity, but never, however desperate she was, would she touch beer. Even among drinkers whose tastes are less extreme, some discrimination usually applies. Many men who feel powerless to control their extreme aggression when insulted by another man have absolute control over their reactions to women, even in the face of direct physical assault: others experience the opposite reactions.

In establishing the significance of the availability of victims, therefore, it is essential to identify those who have been victimised in the past, and to isolate their *necessary* and *sufficient* characteristics. Necessary qualities are those which tend to be shared by victims (for example, being blonde) but which alone do not mean that they will be targeted. Sufficient attributes are those which *must* be present for the behaviour to occur (for example, wearing a short skirt) and which, when present, outweigh other features. Research findings on victim characteristics for various types of offender are likely to highlight additional areas for assessment which might not seem obvious otherwise.

If a chronology (history of significant past acts, in date order) can be established, it may also be possible to observe whether the individual's selection criteria are *broadening* over time to include a more diverse group, or *narrowing* to a more specific range.

As in previous case examples, many offenders are unaware consciously either of the characteristics of the group from which they select victims, or of the reasons behind their selectivity. Some only develop this degree of self-awareness fully in therapy or counselling, but frequently it is during the course of a thorough assessment that patterns start to become clear to them. This emergence of insight, however, is only likely to happen in an unthreatening atmosphere where the professional takes care to suspend value judgement and to encourage *exploratory thinking* by the person concerned. They are already likely to have constructed a set of distorted attitudes about their own behaviour which allows it to continue and protects their self-esteem, attitudes which they will not be courageous enough to challenge in the face of obvious condemnation. It is, of course, fairly easy to make a client/patient say what you want to hear, by giving them clear signs about what is and is not acceptable to you. Regrettably, this tells you everything about how quick they are to catch on, and absolutely nothing about their capacity or desire to modify core beliefs and behaviour. With no accurate baseline, too, there is little chance of measuring real change.

Key questions about victim availability include:

- *What opportunity does the individual have to exercise a normal drive?*
- *How active has the individual been in seeking out victims?*
- *What characteristics are sufficient or necessary for a person to be selected as a victim? What would disqualify them from selection?*
- *Has any action of the individual increased the likelihood of triggering behaviour in a potential victim?*

VICTIM FACTORS

The ability of victims to prevent or limit the harm they suffer varies widely. The Internal/External Drive scale at the beginning of this chapter may be combined with this variable:

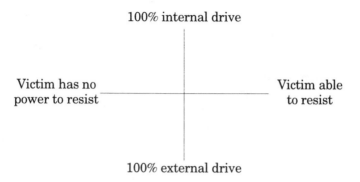

100% internal drive

Victim has no power to resist ——————— Victim able to resist

100% external drive

At one end of the scale, a mugger who attacks his victims from behind and beats them into unconsciousness before robbing them obviously gives no opportunity to resist. At the other, an easily-enraged individual who reacts to perceived slights with the offer of violence, but who may be pacified with a non-aggressive response, allows her potential victim a chance to avoid harm. In between these extremes a would-be child molester, who initiates contact with his victims in the park by offering to show them pornographic pictures, might provide the opportunity for an aware, confident child to walk away from the situation unharmed; a more vulnerable child may be unable to refuse even this fairly blatant trap and the solicitations which follow.

The victim's capacity to resist, therefore, depends on a number of interacting factors, the most significant of which include the style of the aggressive act, the individual victim concerned, and the relationship within which the behaviour occurs.

Behavioural style

The mugging example above involves (a) a self-initiated attack, which (b) is without warning and (c) uses an immediately high level of physical violence against which there is little realistic defence. Harmful acts can vary in all these respects:

(a) Where the victim does nothing to engage their aggressor except to be in the wrong place at the wrong time, or to look or behave in a perfectly normal way, clearly their capacity to change the course of events is reduced. This is because the assault is primarily *self-initiated* (or internally driven) and less amenable to victim influence.

(b) Where the *suddenness of the harm* inflicted gives them no opportunity to respond either verbally or physically, their influence diminishes further. Behaviour which only gradually becomes more suspicious, aversive or threatening may (other factors considered) allow scope for avoidance or counterattack.

(c) Obviously, where a *high level of coercion* is used or threatened, victim influence is severely limited. Extremely powerful forms of coercion may be non-violent, but still represent consequences unacceptable to the victim: threat to a precious relationship is a typical example. A child who is told that they will be sent to a children's home, or a woman who believes that her husband will be informed, may well feel as powerless to resist further abuse as if they had suffered violent coercion. More so, in some cases, because sudden violence can frequently brand the aggressor as socially unacceptable and therefore more likely to be condemned by others: emotional threats can give the impression that it is the victim, not their abuser, who has disqualified themselves from the right to outside support.

The *manner* in which the individual typically inflicts harm becomes especially significant when the potential victim(s) can be readily identified in advance, less so when they are as yet unknown. Based on the 'forewarned is forearmed' principle, the ability of significant others to anticipate, recognise and avoid being victimised can then be assessed and hopefully enhanced to within acceptably safe limits. This is considered in more detail in the next chapter.

Type of victim
Even when the style of the aggressor allows some scope for the victim to avoid, deflect, minimise or repel the assault, some victims will be far more able than others to escape harm. This capacity (or lack of it) may be unpredictable to the perpetrator; challenging strangers to a brawl involves taking the chance that the person challenged may be a karate black-belt, while nocturnal domestic burglary holds the possibility of fierce dogs or an armed householder. At the same time, the opportunistic aggressor risks

the possibility of having selected a far more vulnerable person than they anticipated.

Other victims are chosen specifically because they are perceived as less able to defend themselves. Elderly people robbed in their homes by thieves posing as officials are a well-known example. Some research on the choice of victims by paedophiles has suggested that particular children are far more likely to be targeted than others. When a group of these men were shown videos of children playing in a school playground, they identified as most likely to be singled out and victimised those children who appeared isolated, unhappy, and peripheral to the most popular activities. Families in which a child is clearly marginalised may attract potential abusers through a similar process. Frequently, those who harm such children from within the family report no conscious intention to do so at the beginning; they often identify strongly with their victim, seeing their own early experience reflected in the child's distress and vulnerability. The shift from empathy to exploitation may occur through an inability to set limits to the intimacy created, or through the child's failure to respond as required.

As well as physical vulnerability and emotional insecurity, known previous maltreatment may also increase the chances of further abuse. This may be because the victim is perceived as 'spoilt goods' already and thus not worthy of protection, or because they are seen as less likely to protest actively. They may have a reputation for lying (real or contrived), which further reduces the chances of any complaint being heard. (Well-publicised court decisions over the years against rape victims who have otherwise been sexually active have inevitably reinforced some people's perception that only the unblemished merit full protection.) The influence of the victim on the behaviour of the aggressor certainly deserves careful analysis, (see below) but should not be assumed on the basis of their own history alone.

Relationship with aggressor

It is often said that most people's fear of attacks by strangers are way out of proportion to their statistical probability; most assaults occur against the background of an existing relationship. Even burglary, seemingly one of the most impersonal violations, probably involves parties who are known to each other far more frequently than is realised by the general public.

When determining future risk, understanding the part which

interpersonal dynamics have played in past offences is central, especially where the aggressor, victim and significant others know each other well. Crucially, how much time has it taken to build up the necessary relationship with previous victims? Where established domestic systems have been the setting for harmful behaviour in the past, the likelihood of similarly high-risk environments developing unnoticed are clearly reduced, given reasonable monitoring. The scenario where a transient, superficial encounter has led to harm (for instance, wounding of a taxi driver in the course of an argument over payment) suggests a much higher probability of future impulsive acts of aggression, if similar conditions prevail. The necessary situation is far simpler to set up.

Understanding of the significant *mechanism* operating within the relationship is also essential. Is the behaviour based on a key cognitive distortion on the part of the perpetrator (for example, the belief that anyone on whom they depend is bound to be compulsively unfaithful)? Is it a predictable response on their part to a particular power imbalance between them and their victim? Is there a tendency of one or both parties to create circumstances in which harm is inevitable? (see Chapter 9) It is common, for example, to encounter families where dramatic emotional splitting and alliances are habitual, and where members are seen as either wholly for or wholly against each other; this mechanism can sometimes underlie abuse of one or more individuals. In contrast, other relationships lack appropriate boundaries for intimacy, such that perceived invasion and consequent rejection are familiar triggers.

The *costs to the victim of resistance* will often be closely related to these relationship factors, and will have a powerful influence on their capacity to resist. Often an assessment can pinpoint quite specifically the risky dynamics which undermine the victim (see also Chapter 11), and which would need to be addressed in order for future risk to be contained.

Key questions about the victim's capacity to resist include:

- *How might the style of the assault have significantly impaired resistance?*
- *Was the victim particularly ill-equipped to resist? How obvious would this have been to the perpetrator?*
- *What relationship factors are likely to have militated against resistance?*

VICTIM FACTORS

An assessment of risk also needs to take into account any relevant power issues in past harmful behaviour.

Socially derived power

The term *abuse* implies the imposition of an action by a more powerful person on one of lesser power; an action which is not in the interests of the abused person. Where nature or society has ascribed greater strength or status to one individual, it seems reasonable to assume, all other things being equal, that they are the more powerful. It may be useful, however, to examine the issue of power inequality in a little more depth.

Inequality in a relationship may be of a temporary *or* permanent, partial *or* whole, innate *or* prescribed *nature.*

Temporary inequality exists where the more powerful (dominant) person has some greater skill, knowledge or experience which is to be passed to the less powerful (subordinate) person. The purpose of the relationship is to reduce or eliminate the inequality: thus the pupil becomes as knowledgeable as the teacher, the apprentice gains the skills of the master, the child learns from its parent how to become a parent in turn. *Permanent* inequality exists where there is no such assumption that the relationship is based in service to the subordinate; indeed, the aim may be to increase or consolidate the inequality. Thus, there is no implication that the tenant farmer is being apprenticed to become a landowner, that the colonised nation will be strengthened to the level of the coloniser, nor that the subordinate female is being taught how to be as powerful as her spouse.

Another part of the difference is related to the *part/whole* nature of the inequality; whether the superior/inferior status is seen as integral to the people concerned or merely a result of the situation. For example, in the surgery, the doctor is dominant and the architect, as the patient who benefits from the doctor's greater expertise, the subordinate. When the doctor calls in the architect to design her house, she is in turn takes the subordinate role. When they meet on the tennis court, or in the supermarket, it is likely to be on equal terms. Their inequality is *partial*, and situation-specific; it does not *define* them in terms of their whole identities.

The third important dimension of power inequality is its perceived source. Some individuals' status is *prescribed*; that is, conferred on them by the society in which they live, in the form of class, education, accent, religious group etc. In theory, they can outgrow it or emigrate out of it, the basis of many legends and folk-tales. Moses, Dick Whittington, and the rags-to-riches entrepreneur are all examples of people born into subordinate groups who 'cheated the system' and prospered. For others, subordinate or dominant status is with them immutably from birth. To be born female, disabled, or into a racially disadvantaged group is to inherit one or more of the most enduring subordinate characteristics; these are *innate*.

Personally Derived Power

Social aspects of inequality are relatively well-recognised, as is the potential for abuse between people separated by clear differences in social status. However, it becomes more difficult when those concerned start out, to all extents and purposes, equal. When does sexual exploration between adolescents, for example, become abuse of one young person by another? Is it always the case that the individual with all the prescribed and innate advantages is the abuser?

Having taken into account, therefore, the power discrepancies innately and prescriptively inherent in the background to the relationship, *interpersonal* factors must also be considered. Popularity, intelligence, and physical attractiveness are potentially vital factors, identified in the case example above. Another is emotional stability.

Consider the issue of domestic violence. As previously emphasised, the responsibility for an act is always that of the actor; the victim can, at most, only be an influence. It is well recognised, however, that those who become violent towards their partners are often also highly dependent, often on their victim. Again, the *function* of the behaviour in the relationship must be thoroughly understood in order to predict the possibility of changing it.

In some cases, it may be that the person who is more physically capable of assault is also the most emotionally vulnerable. A thorough assessment should explore the other power dynamics within the relationship before concluding that the victim was completely subordinate and the aggressor wholly dominant on an interpersonal level.

In Chapter 8, evaluation of the *cost of the behaviour* focused on the degree of harm likely to be caused by a repetition of past actions. When the individual(s) who are likely to be targeted

Case Example

A Caucasian boy of 14 and an Asian girl of 11 are discovered to have been indulging in mutual sexual 'petting' and attempted intercourse, for which the boy is initially held to blame. Can you imagine any factors which might lead you to believe that the younger child was in fact the more powerful of the two, and thus more responsible ? Age, gender, racial advantage, and physical size would all indicate that the older child held the more powerful position in the relationship.

In this case, the girl was an extremely bright, attractive and popular member of her peer group, while the boy was in the remedial class in his year, ostracised and ridiculed by his classmates because of his physical appearance and poor coordination. It was clear from more detailed exploration of the relationship dynamics that, while both had consented to the sexual activity, the greater *interpersonal* power was held by the younger child.

have already been identified, the risk assessment will be able to include a prediction of *applied cost*, in other words, the vulnerability of a **particular person** in relation to the specified act:

> *Thus, a behaviour which in isolation may be regarded as high- or low-cost may need to be re-evaluated in the light of those individuals who are likely to be exposed to it.*

For example, a person known to suffer relapses of mental illness in prolonged situations of emotional stress is likely to be more affected than most by the fairly mild anger control problems of a potential flatmate. A child who has already suffered extreme distress through witnessing parental violence may be considered unable to tolerate any further exposure to such behaviour.

Where no likely victims can be identified, (perhaps because the placement for the foreseeable future offers no clear opportunity for harm), the risk assessment should take into account the cost to an averagely robust victim, and identify any victim characteristics which would *increase* the cost.

ELEVEN

RELIABILITY OF DETECTION

Most risk assessments lead to the conclusion that there is some defined probability of the behaviour occurring in the future, with the foreseeable cost to the victim likely to fall within a certain range. In some circumstances, this information will form a sufficient basis for decisions about placement, legal proceedings, protection plans etc to be made. If a court is informed that an armed robber is highly likely to reoffend, that the potential degree of violence is considerable, and that treatment is or is not likely to reduce the risk significantly, then its course of action will be fairly clear. In other cases, an additional set of factors needs to be included in the equation.

Case Example

Two women have in the past caused significant injuries to their children when clinically depressed. They are currently receiving drug treatment which in both cases has controlled the depression effectively, but there are concerns that external stressors might render this control unreliable in the future. From past evidence it seems that, early in the slide into depression, both women lose insight into the severity of their mental state and its implications for their children's safety.

One of the women is regularly visited by a health visitor and a Community Psychiatric Nurse, and the children receive weekly check-ups from the school nurse, with whom they have a warm and confiding relationship. The other woman leads a rather itinerant lifestyle, often leaving home with the children for days or weeks at a time to attend festivals or to stay with friends around the country. These absences tend to occur on the spur of the moment, often when

she feels low and in need of stimulation, and professionals
are rarely informed of when or where the family has gone
until they return.
    While the probability of relapse is essentially the same for
both women, clearly the risk of harm is higher in the family
which is less amenable to monitoring.

Professionals' confidence in their *ability to detect* an increase
in risk level, or *to identify the earliest recurrence* of harmful
behaviour, is therefore a vital factor in many applied
assessments.

URGENCY VERSUS COST

In each individual case, it is necessary to decide how essential it
is to detect any of the following:

(a) The first signs of any increase in risk?
(b) Specified high-risk indicators?
(c) The first harmful incident?
(d) Duration of a harmful pattern beyond a reasonable period
     (eg a week/6 months)?

The critical factors in the degree of urgency which applies are
the *speed with which risk will escalate* and the *likely cost* to the
individuals concerned.

In the case of a normally gentle young man suffering from
manic-depression, who when actively manic has nearly killed his
father, (a) would probably apply. The potential cost of his
becoming ill again is too high for even a minor relapse to be
tolerated. Particularly, if he is known to become very ill extremely
quickly, the first signs of relapse would be the trigger for
immediate intervention.

In (b), a person who has committed sexual offences against
children may normally experience fluctuations in her child-
related fantasies, which she has learned to manage
appropriately. However, she has become aware that a strong
impulse to re-establish contact with a paedophile group is a
reliable warning sign that her deviant drive is starting to spiral
dangerously, and that she needs to contact her therapist without
delay.

An example of (c) could be a family where child neglect occurs
during periods of parental discord, and where the intervention

strategy might be triggered by the first unexplained absence of the child from school. Harm, technically, has already occurred at this stage, but it is considered tolerable if swift action is taken to prevent further deterioration.

Where *(d)* applies, clearly either the cost is low, or the potential for professional intervention limited. An example might be a return to a heavy drinking pattern in response to a bereavement, where the only likely victim is the drinker herself, and where there is a reasonable chance that she will be able to regain stability within a certain period without outside help. In the meantime, compulsory treatment is not a legal option.

A comprehensive analysis along relapse prevention lines (see Chapter 7) will have identified High Risk Factors; those internal or external events which increase the probability of the behaviour happening. The individual may have a repertoire of tactics for avoiding and/or managing these risky situations.... but sometimes these tactics fail. When this happens, or when risk unexpectedly emerges from another direction, some warning system needs to be triggered if the situation is to be contained within acceptable limits.

In many cases, the individual concerned is in the best position to alert others to increased risk. Where they cannot do this (for example, through lack of understanding or low self-awareness), others have to act as monitors and informants. Regardless of who is responsible for the warning process, in order to carry it out effectively they need *(i) to know what to look for* and *(ii) to be confident that reporting of the warning sign is in their best interests*. The suspicion that being frank could bring about catastrophic punishment is hardly an inducement to self-disclosure, but sadly many people in a risky situation fear precisely this. A mentally ill person who knows from experience that relapse means lengthy readmission to hospital and disintegration of her normal life may well try to hide symptoms from her doctor. A family in which physical abuse has occurred may be tempted to cover up a recurrence of violence because they cannot bear to risk the removal of the violent but much-loved family member.

Others may feel unable to distinguish confidently between risky and non-risky factors (for example, between appropriate and inappropriate physical contact), and be reluctant to report their concerns for fear of 'crying Wolf'. It is not unknown for monitoring professionals to be similarly confused about what constitutes a low- or high-risk warning sign; the natural inclination in this situation is to be over-inclusive, and react too dramatically. Predictably, this tends to reduce the reliability of subsequent reporting.

Understanding of *significant* warning signs in an individual case is therefore essential. Most will be identified during assessment, and added to during the monitoring phase as new situations arise. Others can often be suggested through relevant research into the specific condition or behaviour. Pioneering work into the early signs of relapse in schizophrenia, for example, has provided a checklist of commonly-experienced phenomena, and encourages the person concerned (and those closest to them) to identify other, more idiosyncratic, signs too. The procedure then tests out the predictive accuracy of the signs, and the ability of those involved to spot them promptly, by noting which occur and are reported in the next relapse. Through this process, recurrence of illness is detected at the earliest possible stage. This means that it can be treated far more quickly, often through a minimal increase in antipsychotic medication, rather than deteriorating to the point where drastic measures like hospitalisation are necessary. It is easy to see how mental health professionals, from being perceived as spying saboteurs, might become reassuring figures engaged in a shared commitment to the patient's quality of life. Members of a family who have previously resisted outside interference can often prove valuable allies, once they feel in control of at least part of a comprehensible process of supervision and protection.

A similar structure can be developed to predict and manage potential harm which is not related to illness.

Case Example

A Family Centre team had been asked to assess a man with a horrific history of sexual assaults on children, and who for the past 8 years, unknown to Social Services, had been living in the area with his wife and daughter now 7 years old. As there was no indication that any abuse had occurred within the family, there was felt to be insufficient grounds to ask him to leave the household, and instead a risk management package was put in place, using the Relapse Prevention approach.

After thorough assessment, Low, Medium and High Risk

Factors, and the equivalent warning signs, were identified. The team drew up a contract with the family, making it clear exactly what events they would expect to be told about, by whom, and what response the family could expect from them in each instance.

(The team's agreed responses had of course been discussed with and approved by their managers in advance, which in itself was felt to be an extremely instructive and thought-provoking process.)

OPENNESS TO MONITORING

For an event to be monitored with confidence, of course, it has to be possible to tell whether it has or hasn't happened.

Where a high degree of confidence is necessary, this tends to mean that practitioners will be doing the monitoring directly themselves, and that the behaviour (or its effects) will need to be *observable* or *measurable*. Where a mother's ability to care for her child safely is dependent on her abstaining from drugs, for example, frequent blood tests are usually carried out as part of the monitoring process. Where the past harm has been severe physical abuse of an elderly, dementing person by their carer, regular physical examinations would be standard.

A critical factor in such cases, therefore, will be the willingness of the assessed individual and/or those around them to submit to the necessary checks.

Case Example

A man who had killed one of his young children while suffering from paranoid schizophrenia wished to return to the family home after his illness had been successfully controlled with oral medication. His family were equally eager for his return. Both he and his wife expressed full support for the Clinical Team's recommendation that he should continue with the drug treatment indefinitely in order to reduce the risk of relapse.

However, when the need for regular blood tests to check drug levels was explained to them, they refused to comply, saying that they resented the slur on their integrity. In response the Team proposed that the man should have his treatment by injection rather than tablets, an option which was also politely refused. While the couple appeared to accept the role that mental illness had played in their child's death, it became clear that they were actually very ambivalent about the cause and its solution. Subsequent psychological work with them revealed that they had gone along with professional opinion to avoid open conflict, but privately believed that the fatal assault had been the result merely of 'overwork'. Between themselves, they had decided that there was no need to continue with medication following discharge from hospital.

Despite the absence of any symptoms of psychosis, therefore, the Clinical Team's recommendation was that the man should not be allowed to return home because of the inadequacy of monitoring procedures.

This example underlines how useful it can be to make use of objective measures, even when compliance does not seem to be in doubt. This is particularly desirable in the early stages of monitoring, and may be reintroduced during high-risk periods.

CAPACITY OF OTHERS TO REPORT AND PROTECT

When a less exacting degree of confidence is required (perhaps where the anticipated cost is less, or where the probability is reduced after a period of improved control), monitoring by those personally involved may alone be sufficient. This may also be acceptable even with high-cost risks, if reporting reliability has been demonstrated to be so high that objective evidence does not need to be routinely collected by professionals.

Sometimes it happens that the potential victim is the only person in a position to respond to early warning signs; for instance, in the case of domestic violence in a two-person household where the perpetrator is not a good informant. In addition to the factors previously highlighted (knowledge about what to look for, and confidence in the professional response), the informant's *capacity* to act appropriately should also be evaluated. Even when the identified informant is not the likely victim, they may well be constrained by factors which are not immediately obvious. There are many reasons why a person who can see the danger signs and knows that help is at hand may yet feel unable to speak out.

RISK ASSESSMENT

ACCEPTANCE OF COST OF BEHAVIOUR

It is important to establish that those in a monitoring role understand how seriously the behaviour is viewed by professionals, and why. Sometimes, when everyone concerned agrees that an incident must not recur, it is easy to assume that they agree for the same reasons.

Case Example

A Child Protection Case Conference was reaching its final stages, having considered the risk to a teenage boy whose mother had admitted inciting him to have sex with her. It seemed clear that the boy's father was committed to ending the abuse, and had agreed to stringent guidelines about sleeping arrangements, privacy, limit-setting etc, and the boy's return home seemed imminent.

A social worker new to the case asked the apparently basic question 'Why is it so important that no further sexual activity should take place between your son and his mother?' To the dismay of all present, the man answered 'Because if she gets pregnant, the baby may be born handicapped'. Despite all the work that had been undertaken up until then (and his proven ability to repeat the social workers' arguments), he had remained fixed in his simplistic views of what was actually wrong with his wife's behaviour.

As discussed in previous chapters, full appreciation of all the costs is not *necessarily* a pre-requisite of effective monitoring and prevention. Parents who are committed to stopping their teenage son's joyriding may do so purely because they want to keep him from further arrests, and not through any desire to protect other road-users. Assuming that they sincerely want him to stop (as opposed to wanting him to stop getting caught), their preventative strategy may be just as effective as one based on more altruistic motives. *In general, however, the more complex the behaviour, and the more subtle the ways in which harm can be caused, the more important it is for cooperation to be based on comprehension.*

Acknowledgement of future risk

The implication of the above example of incest was of course that, believing only intercourse to be harmful, the father was not likely to recognise the full significance of other sexual acts between his wife and son. His capacity to report and protect against future harm would be compromised by his understanding of the wider effects of past behaviour.

In other cases, the seriousness of previous conduct may be fully appreciated, but the likelihood of its recurrence greatly underestimated. In the earlier example of the man who had killed his child when actively mentally ill, both parents were tragically aware of the enormity of their loss. At the same time, they believed that a minor re-adjustment of their lifestyle would be sufficient to eliminate all future risk. In the same way as an offender is often convinced that a fervent desire not to reoffend will be enough to overcome long-established patterns of behaviour or powerful drives, those around them may also predict the future according to their hopes rather than their experience.

This is of course very understandable on a number of levels. A relationship which has been devastated by one person's actions, and is painfully being rebuilt, will generally benefit from trust and optimism, not negative thinking and suspicion. Few couples, for example, trying to save their marriage after one of them has been unfaithful, would feel that formal surveillance devices such as electronic tagging and compulsory curfews would play a useful part in the delicate reconstruction process. Most would probably try to *behave as if* they believed that further trust was justified, until such time as pretence was no longer necessary.

It is not really surprising, therefore, that so many people who have good reason to fear destructive behaviour from those close to them *appear* to believe it unlikely. Sensitive enquiry can often distinguish between those who are genuinely deceiving themselves and those who just cannot imagine how realism and hope can be combined in practice. Typical of those in the second category was the woman who said 'I feel like I have to choose between having faith in my son and condemning him as a liability for ever'. As emphasised earlier, it is crucial that a distinction is always stressed between the *person* (their worth as a human being, their strengths, virtues and needs) and the *behaviour* (its history, influences, probability and costs). Where devoted supporters recognise that the assessed individual is respected as more than just the sum of their problems, they are likely to feel able to express their fears more freely.

It can be useful to draw up, with the help of the individual and those close to them, a provisional timetable of strategies. In the short term, most people are able to accept fairly rigorous safeguards (even those externally imposed and objectively monitored) if they can also foresee how these might become more informal and under their own control over time. Again, the keystone of genuine 'compliance' is handing back to those concerned the knowledge and power to protect themselves and others to the full extent of their ability.

Ultimately, genuine acknowledgment of future risk can only be assumed where it is accompanied by a willingness to work with a reasonable protection strategy.

In cases where not even lip-service is paid to the possibility of future risk, it is of course highly unlikely that those concerned will comply with attempts at supervision or prevention. There are exceptions, however, even to this fairly obvious rule. A family who vigorously reject the suggestion that harm could recur, or even deny the obvious guilt of one member, can occasionally cooperate with a protection plan with a thoroughness that reveals their unspoken concerns. Often this indicates that one or more of them is too emotionally fragile to accept the truth openly, but that complying with 'unnecessary' precautions imposed from outside brings reassurance and relief without the need for confrontation. Where risk reduction, rather than absolute prevention, is the goal, this may well be an acceptable compromise. It can also in some cases provide an atmosphere where more open and honest communication can develop, once the immediate threat to the key individual is seen to have receded.

While familiarity usually leads to *under-estimation* of risk, occasionally those closest to the person appear to have a wildly *inflated* view of their riskiness. Since this may arise from some as-yet-undisclosed knowledge, it is always worthy of careful investigation. Where it is apparently unfounded, over-suspiciousness should be assessed as a potential influence on risk in its own right. It is not uncommon for significant others to 'set up' the individual, consciously or otherwise, to repeat the destructive behaviour; usually this serves to maintain a wider maladaptive pattern in key relationships.

Case Example

A young woman with learning difficulties had on several occasions picked up other people's babies from their prams in the village high street and attempted to walk off with them. She was easily apprehended each time, and it was judged that no harm had been intended, but naturally her conduct had caused enormous distress. The risk assessment carried out by the Forensic Psychiatric Team had indicated that a primary drive behind her actions was a need to feel like a competent adult, with status and a productive role, in contrast to the passive, childlike existence she had led since leaving school.

A multi-agency core group, which included the young woman and her parents, devised a plan of increasing responsibility and stimulation outside the home, with monitoring by professionals being gradually withdrawn as time went on. Despite great initial success, however, her behaviour took an abrupt turn for the worse shortly after she had proudly managed to travel alone to and from her new job. The core group members fretted as they checked through the formulation and the plan; had they misread her apparent need for autonomy? Had things moved too fast for her confidence? Suspicions were aroused, however, by the parents' rather smug reaction to the set-back; they had 'known all along' that she wasn't safe to be out alone. Further discussions with the young woman revealed that, travelling to work, she had spotted her father discreetly following her several days running, and had been furious at what she perceived as a conspiracy to deceive her by everyone concerned.

The parents eventually admitted that they had been unable to tolerate the anxiety generated by her progress, and couldn't resist falling back into their old, over-protective ways. The core group acknowledged that not enough weight had been given to the parents' fears and shame about their daughter's past behaviour, and the plan was modified to provide them with greater reassurance and support from the wider village community for 'letting go'.

Vigilance

Vigilance in this context refers to *the ability to remain alert to risk indicators,* even where they differ superficially from those expected, and when considerable time has passed since the harmful event. It will clearly be difficult to measure this fully in the initial assessment, especially when those concerned have not been required to be vigilant in the past; it will need to be monitored over time.

Where the warning signs (and the principles behind them) are understood, their significance acknowledged, and the professionals' likely response welcomed, readiness to report is rarely a problem. It is worth considering those factors which can reduce vigilance, all the same.

Time alone is an erosive influence in matters of judgement. Take an unwelcome event like the chimney catching fire. Once it has happened to you, your feelings about using the fire change dramatically. You treat it with exaggerated respect, watch what you put on it, keep the flames low, check on it from time to time and probably have the chimney cleaned more frequently over the next few years than is really necessary. As time passes, though, and nothing else goes wrong, it is difficult to maintain this level of alertness. The following are likely to occur:

- As the memory of the event becomes less vivid, so does your sense *not only of its seriousness but also of the likelihood of its happening again*. This erosion probably happens more at the emotional level than the intellectual.
- You will tend to *over-emphasise differences between past and current circumstances*; ('we've had a few mild winters lately; I haven't used it as regularly as I did then'), or *emphasise new awareness* ('of course, I don't have great blazing fires like I used to') or *external protection* ('chimney sweeps these days leave far less soot behind'). While all these observations may be valid in themselves, the basic truth, that it was a horrible experience which can easily happen to you, becomes less compelling.
- *Complacency eventually tends to outweigh anxiety*, particularly as you observe how other people who are far less careful appear to be problem-free. Unless you are the obsessive sort of person who sticks rigidly to all self-imposed rules, you can end up behaving much as you did before, with a corresponding increase in risk.

One of the factors in the erosion of vigilance is a *lack of certainty about the specific causes of the original incident*. If you don't know precisely why the chimney caught fire when it did, you will tend to be superstitiously over-cautious in all details, the irrelevant as well as the crucial. When you discover that most of your precautions make no difference, you are far more likely to relax the ones that do. If an offender is warned to make 10 major changes to his lifestyle in order to minimise the chances of reoffending, and over time discovers that he can flout 9 of them without any obvious ill-effects, he is unlikely to remain vigilant in upholding the 10th, and vital, one.

It is therefore unhelpful in the long run for professionals to impose more restrictions than are really necessary, or to imply that all are equally important, when they do not really know if this is the case. In uncertainty, it is more useful to engage the individual and/or others in testing out the causal relationships between factors, in controlled circumstances if necessary. This sort of involvement is likely to increase the vigilance of all concerned.

Case Example

Following a suicide attempt, a young single mother was treated with anti-depressant medication and cognitive therapy in hospital. She participated actively in risk-reduction work which focused on triggers for low mood and early signs of relapse; it seemed evident that the original, external causes of her depression were no longer present in her life.

On follow-up at home, she complained of feeling sluggish and unable to function adequately, and over the next 2 years, asked repeatedly for a reduction in her drug dosage, arguing that she wanted a chance to see if she could cope using only the non-medical techniques. This was resisted by her GP, on the principle that the cost to her children was too great should she become depressed again. She reluctantly continued to take the drug, but lost her rapport with the professionals involved and adopted an increasingly passive role in her own monitoring.

In time, however, a new doctor who was more receptive to her views, supported the plan for a phased reduction in her medication. Several possible strategies were drawn up, including voluntary hospital admission for a defined period, with care arranged for the children. 6 months later, she was drug-free and enjoying improved relationships with those supervising her. Within 18 months, she had proved herself reliable enough to monitor her own mood and had handled several minor crises proactively. Five years on, she is the founder and organiser of a depression self-help group, and is training as an advocate for people with mental health problems.

The woman in the above example became a strong advocate of the principle that people should be actively involved in the management of their own difficulties. It is becoming increasingly well-recognised that one of the damaging side-effects of professional intervention is *a paralysis of the individual's own capacity to recover* in a way suited to the life they still have to live. It is hardly worth making an effort to remain alert with regard to your weaknesses when someone else is paid to do it for you (or to you), and furthermore, has a qualification in it. *Over-control* by professionals is often a significant factor in reduced vigilance by those monitoring risk.

Finally, a word on *general versus specific* vigilance; the ability to recognise warning signs which differ slightly from anticipated ones. A problem in 'learning from experience' is that life rarely leaves its banana skins in exactly the same spot next time. If the lesson learnt is too specific, it can protect us only from a very narrow range of hazards. This underlines how useful it is for those monitoring risk to be aware of the general principles behind it, rather than just the individual warning signs and triggers which operated before. Some people have a limited capacity to make such generalisations themselves, and may need numerous specific examples to illustrate the range of situations which deserve monitoring.

Case Example

The mother of a child who was considered to be at risk had been warned to watch out for her new partner's tendency to portray the child as dishonest. (This had been a consistent antecedent in his previous offending against children.) When the child subsequently told workers that her family had stopped believing what she told them, and it became clear that the offender was responsible, the mother was asked how she had allowed this to influence her. 'But he never once called her a liar' she protested; 'in fact whenever he came and told me that other people had caught her telling lies, he always said that he didn't believe it himself. He was always standing up for her, even when it was ridiculous!' She had assumed, in a concrete way, that she had to guard against outright accusations, whereas the threat had actually taken the form of a more subtle erosion of her confidence in her daughter.

Power to intercede or report

> *Even when there is a sincere desire to prevent harm, when principles of risk are understood and the warning signs*

or first incident of harm recognised, those concerned may still not be able to act appropriately to prevent further incidents or to alert others.

The reason for such powerlessness, of course, is usually fear, in its many forms. The example which probably comes most readily to mind is that of a victim who fears *direct reprisal* from their abuser more than they fear the continued abuse. The threat from the aggressor in other cases may not be that of direct retribution, but *dependency-related*. Many victims are well aware that their report of further abuse will lead to immediate relief, but cannot tolerate the anticipated loss of a person on whom they are emotionally or materially dependent. In my experience, this type of fear is the key factor in the majority of failures to report, even where active coercion also applies.

A more subtle pressure may be exerted, sometimes unknowingly, by those who are neither the aggressor nor the principal victim. Many a child has continued to suffer abuse from one parent, knowing that help is at hand, because they perceived that disclosure would be unbearable to the other. A little girl, who for years had been sexually assaulted by her older brother, explained that the boy was her parents' favourite, and that getting him into trouble 'would make them hate me more than ever'. An elderly man in a nursing home who knew that his friend was suffering victimisation at the hands of the Matron was convinced by his fellow residents that if he reported the brutality, the home would be closed and they would all be sent to the hospital geriatric ward. A ex-Broadmoor patient who informed his mother that he was about to tell his Community Psychiatric Nurse about the return of his hallucinations was warned that 'if you bring all that lot down on us again it'll kill your Dad'. This was particularly ironic (and effective) as his father had in the past been the victim of his most serious psychotic episode.

Assessment of these insidious influences often has to be approached hypothetically, if it is to avoid triggering the very fear that the individual is seeking to prevent. 'Why are you afraid of admitting that X has occurred?' will probably be experienced as acutely threatening. 'Can you think of a reason why someone knowing about X might not want to talk about it?' may well open the door to cautious confidences. Tempting though it may be to promise that the dreaded consequence will not occur, of course, such a guarantee is rarely within the gift of the assessor. Reassurances that 'of course Daddy won't go to prison/the others won't hate you/ you won't be taken into care/ the world won't collapse' might help to gain an incriminating account, but the cost to the informant if the worst does happen could be quite devastating. At the very least, the confidence of the deceived person will be undermined to the extent that the reliability of their future reporting is severely compromised.

Key questions to be addressed in relation to the reliability of detection include:

- *What needs to be detected; the first warning sign? Serious risk indicators? The first harmful incident?*
- *Does everyone know what the professional response to each level of incident will be?*
- *Is the urgency or potential cost such that outside monitoring is essential? Is this enforceable in practice?*
- *Are 'significant others' reliable enough to contain the risk? Aware of seriousness? Acknowledging probability? Able to recognise signs? Cooperative with protection strategy? Vigilant? Able to report?*
- *Has everything been done to facilitate reporting?*

SECTION FOUR

THE OVERVIEW

TWELVE

RISK ASSESSMENT CHECKLIST

This chapter summarises the main functions of each section in a full risk assessment, with suggestions about what might be included in each. Not all assessments will need to be this comprehensive, of course; some will have a very narrow focus, others will be supplementary to work already done, and in many cases the information necessary to complete areas of the assessment will simply not exist. The summary is intended, therefore, as a rapid means of checking that all that *can* be done *has* been done, and as a prompt to identify areas of deliberate omission or the absence of data.

THE RISK ASSESSMENT FRAMEWORK

- **POSSIBLE SOURCES OF BIAS**
  Related to the client/patient
  Related to the assessor
  Related to the agency/climate

RISK ASSESSMENT CHECKLIST

- **ASSESSMENT OF INDIVIDUAL RISK**

- DEFINITION OF THE TARGET BEHAVIOUR

- PROBABILITY OF RECURRENCE

- PAST BEHAVIOUR
  Type & Frequency
  Actuarial Prediction

- MOTIVATIONAL DRIVE
  Formulation (including typologies)
  Mental illness/emotional state
  Influence of previous learning
  Necessary triggers/conditions
  Sources of reinforcement
  Deviant *versus* Normal drive

- CONTROLS & DISINHIBITORS
  Existing moral code
  Empathy with victim/s
  Intellectual understanding of issues
  Cognitive distortion
  Impulsivity
  Substance Abuse

- INSIGHT INTO PAST OFFENDING
  Recognition of drive
  Acceptance of risk cycle
  Acknowledgement of future risk
  Motivational stage

- COST OF THE BEHAVIOUR
  To the potential victim(s)
  To the assessed
  To the assessor

- **ASSESSMENT OF APPLIED RISK**

- EMOTIONAL/SOCIAL ENVIRONMENT
  Significant Others
  Intimate relationships
  Sub-cultural influences
  Situational Triggers
  Ambient Factors
  Precipitating Factors

- VICTIM FACTORS
  Availability
  Capacity to resist
  Behavioural style
  Type of victim
  Relationship with aggressor
  Power discrepancy
  Socially derived
  Personally derived
  Influence and Responsibility

- APPLIED COST

- RELIABILITY OF DETECTION
  Urgency *versus* cost
  Presence of early warning signs
  Openness to monitoring
  Capacity of others to protect
  Consequences of disclosure
  Acceptance of seriousness of past behaviour
  Acknowledgement of future risk
  Recognition of need for protective strategy
  Vigilance
  Power to intercept/report

SUMMARY OF RISK

Probability of behaviour recurring   High
Significant
Low

Cost of behaviour recurring   High
Significant
Low

Sources of possible error   Towards over-prediction
Towards under-prediction

Early warning signs   To high risk signs
To significant risk signs
To low risk signs

Agreed professional response
to warning signs   To high risk signs
To significant risk signs
Low risk signs

Level of monitoring   Anticipated time scale
Factors necessary for
relaxation of monitoring

THIRTEEN

PRESENTING YOUR CONCLUSIONS

GENERAL GUIDELINES FOR REPORT WRITING

1. Specify the purpose of the report

Make it clear what your role is, and what you have been asked to do.

For example, in the course of a Child Protection procedure, professionals may be:

- providing a general psychological profile of a parent; investigating specific allegations,
- directly evaluating parenting skills; assessing ability to learn new skills,
- identifying psychological obstacles to change; describing family dynamics,
- monitoring adherence to an interim protection plan,
- predicting future harm,
- commenting on procedures already used,
- making decisions on future placement.

...and that's without any assessment of the child!

If you feel that your role has not been clearly enough defined, ask for a more specific brief. If none is forthcoming, claim in your report a role which you feel is reasonable, given your qualifications and experience, and suggest what else needs doing and who should be doing it, if you know.

A very precise explanation of the assessment and reporting process is also the right of the individual being assessed. Make it clear (in writing if appropriate) whose property the report will be, who will see it, and whether or not the individual has any right to ask for data to be excluded. Some people confuse the role of a clinical assessor in particular with that of a therapist, and may believe that they can confide in them things which they do not want others to know.

Many professionals are unaware of the precise extent of their rights over their own work. Where a solicitor instructs an expert witness to prepare a report, the document becomes the property of the assessed person, via their solicitor. The author retains some rights over its contents, similar to publishing copyright. (If you buy a record, for instance, you own the plastic disc and are entitled to make an ashtray out of it if you want, but the author and publisher have rights over the re-recording of the songs, the lyrics etc.) The solicitor has the right to suppress the report in many cases, and you and your colleagues do not automatically have the right to refer to the material in a subsequent matter concerning that person. An exception may be where there is felt to be a risk to a child, when adverse reports cannot be suppressed by the defence lawyers.

There is also an duty of the assessor to declare whether their professional obligations extend beyond the formal assessment role. Imagine that you are interviewing a young car thief in order to recommend an appropriate disposal to the court, and he reveals in the course of the interview that his father is sexually abusing his young sister. It is probably peripheral to the matter in hand, but are you still constrained (by your contract of employment, for example) to report it independently? These quandaries usually arise in the most unlikely situations, so it is good practice to address them routinely before the start of *any* interview.

2. Ensure data protection

As the author, you have at least some responsibility to ensure that the report is not used inappropriately on this or future occasions. Some agencies already state on certain documents the confidentiality limits which apply, and who may and may not see them. (Social Services are in general more advanced in this practice than the Health Service.) However, in the climate of multi-disciplinary practice it is important to establish how all the agencies involved in the case use documentation in their possession. Some, for example, follow the deplorable practice of making available not only their own paperwork but also that of other professionals, without the consent of the person who has written it. This being the case, you may well wish to add extra safeguards and restrictions of your own. My own reports tend to carry the proviso: 'This report must not be copied, quoted or shown to anyone without the permission of the author'. This of course includes the person about whom it has been written.

While the vast majority of assessments are written with the intention that the assessed person should see and benefit from it, some may actually be harmful if used in this way. A report to court highlighting the deficits of someone who already has fragile self-esteem, for instance, may to be counter-productive to their well-being. As a general rule, where a report cannot be shown to its subject, a companion document which they *can* see should also be produced, making the same points as far as possible, but phrased in a way which provides a constructive basis for therapeutic and other work.

3. Quote sources

Avoid stating as fact anything which cannot be verified beyond reasonable doubt, and state your sources. Old reports can appear preposterously naive in the light of wider knowledge or later events, where they claim 'He no longer fantasises about children', 'She had a happy childhood', 'He drinks only in moderation' or 'She has finally resolved all difficulties in her marriage'. It can seem cumbersome to keep repeating '*Apparently*', '*by his account*', '*it seems that*', '*she reports that*', but to do less is to claim a truth of which you cannot be sure. Being found to be inaccurate in descriptive or historical points weakens others' confidence in your professional judgement by association.

In quoting from other professionals' reports, again the principle 'Trust everyone, but cut the cards' applies. Always give them acknowledgement for their quoted opinions and bear in mind that they may be wrong. If they are, what implication does that have for your own conclusions? It can be useful to refer directly to this inter-relatedness; for example, 'I should emphasise that my assessment of likely future risk rests largely on Dr J's opinion that Ms K was clinically depressed at the time of the offence'.

As well as listing your sources, don't forget to mention those people you approached but who failed to respond, had shredded their records etc. Indicate what part their contribution might have played in your findings.

In describing your own assessment, name the procedures used, whether or not they are standardised on a larger population, and what they are generally used for. As a constraint against over-stating the power of the procedure or the significance of the results, imagine that an opposing barrister has employed an eminent member of your profession to look over your report and to offer criticism!

4. Be theory-driven

One of the factors which distinguishes a professional from lay people is a knowledge of the relevant theory and research in their area of expertise. In order to carry out a risk assessment of a particular harmful behaviour, a good theoretical understanding of this type of conduct is absolutely essential. (If you don't have it, don't be pressurised into carrying out any aspects of the assessment which are beyond your competence. To do so is likely to put you at risk yourself; that of being accused of professional malpractice. If managers or others insist that you do the work, make a written statement of your limitations with respect to the task, and state what training you feel would be necessary to enable you to complete competently what is being asked of you.)

Where possible, it is preferable to have access to *actuarial* data, and to quote it where applicable. If research shows that 65% of individuals of this type, or in this situation, behave in a certain way, then mention this. If the figure can possibly be misinterpreted, clarify it; eg 'While Mr G has demonstrated 4 of the 5 High Risk Indicators identified by Smith & Bloggs, he is still less likely than not to commit this act. Most individuals with all 5 Indicators never behave in this way.'

Then go on to say how the individual in question *differs from the group* on whom the research was based, or what the limitations must be in applying these findings to this case. For example 'The existing research has tended to involve sentenced prisoners, and as yet little has been carried out using a remanded sample. Inferences must therefore be tentative'; or 'The majority of these studies on Afro-Caribbean children have been carried out in the USA. Research in other areas suggests that the reactions of Afro-Caribbean children in Britain are more similar to those of British Caucasian children than they are to their racial counterparts in America. If so, then one would expect the figure to be nearer x'; or 'However, it should be noted that Ms A had voluntarily confessed to the offence, which is unusual in this type of case. It may be assumed, therefore, that she is not entirely typical of this group of offenders'.

Theory which applies to *types of motivational drive* or *categories of perpetrator* is sometimes expressed in the form of **Typologies**. Those best supported by research should be referred to where possible, but where professional experience differs from the theory, make this clear; eg 'Published research on the motivations for shoplifting identifies Types A, B, C & D, while clinical experience would also suggest E & F'. (If you do need to make this sort of comment, it's probably time you were publishing something yourself!)

Keeping up to date with research
Many practitioners, recognising that research-awareness is not part of their professional heritage (or has just been neglected under other pressures), have thought up ways of injecting it fairly painlessly into their routine. Here are some of them:

- *Making more use of information officers.* Previously known as librarians, most agencies have one at district level at least. They have encyclopaedic knowledge of the classic and new materials in their own and other libraries, and are usually distressingly under-used. Most can be persuaded to present regular talks on the resources available; some will even research and present particular topics of interest to groups of staff, and all should trawl the literature for individual references if asked nicely.
- *Using study leave imaginatively.* Most of us only take study leave for formal training or conferences, but some enterprising teams have negotiated the right to use it for 'Peer Updates'. Often in pairs, they will spend one or two days at the service Headquarters or University library, scanning for review papers and other important works on a chosen topic. (Warning the librarian of intentions in advance can lead to some welcome bonuses on arrival!)

    They then summarise 'the state of the art' on that topic in a brief handout, which they may present at a team meeting, interest group or luncheon club, and circulate around the teams/individuals involved in the scheme.
- *Organising outside speakers.* One Child and Family team, painfully aware that their annual training budget could only allow them to send 3.5 people on a one-day course, arranged a deal with equivalent teams in 2 neighbouring counties. They blew their whole budget on bringing in the country's leading authority on child physical abuse, and invited their

colleagues to attend for the day; they in turn attended two other top quality workshop days later in the year, for free.

Other departments/teams have negotiated reciprocal case presentations and lectures with others, bartering in order to avoid the financial constraints altogether.

While it is a professional's duty to have an awareness of current thinking in their field, the actual knowledge gained is often of secondary benefit in comparison to the boost in confidence achieved. One Probation Officer, having spent a day familiarising herself with the latest research on adolescent car theft, described 'the uplifting sense of being in the front line of the profession rather than slogging away blindly in the ranks!' She commented that one of the greatest benefits of the exercise was the confirmation that her current practice was well supported by the latest theories.

5. Describing probability

In the final section of a Risk Assessment, the way that probabilities are worded is extremely important. It is perhaps reasonable to assume that a full and precise report speaks for itself, but it is most often the concluding paragraphs which carry the most weight, and which return to haunt the writer when events turn out contrary to expectations.

Few assessors would be prepared to offer a prediction of 'No Risk', for obvious reasons. *Everyone represents a risk, in the sense that they are theoretically capable of causing harm.* The only runners on whom bookmakers ever refuse to take bets are the out-and-out favourites, after all; even the most hopeless outsiders have odds quoted for them. More pragmatically, though, such a prediction leaves the professional open to scathing and quite avoidable condemnation if proved wrong. In the search for someone to blame after disaster has occurred, the person who has blithely asserted 'No Risk' rather than 'Low Risk unless A, B or C should occur, when probability would increase' will be a sitting duck.

In the absence of statistical descriptors, some form of arbitrary divisions must be used. These vary according to personal preference and custom; I prefer 'High/Significant/Low', to describe probability and cost separately. Reasons should be summarised; eg `The primary drive in his past offending appears to have been delusional, when psychotically depressed. He is currently refusing medication, which in the past has led to a relapse in his mental state within 3 weeks. In my judgement, therefore, while the cost of the behaviour recurring remains low, the probability must currently be seen as high.'

State the future circumstances in which your overall prediction of probability would be increased or reduced; eg 'This estimate is heavily dependent on Ms C's continued abstinence from alcohol; any relapse would, given past behaviour, severely jeopardise her controls'.

6. State the limitations of the report

Your predictions can only be as valid as the information on which they are based; make sure your inferences reflect this. *There is no evidence that...*' is a grand claim, but *'According to the information available to me, there is no evidence...'* is more realistic, and allows the possibility that conflicting facts may arise later. Sometimes it may be feasible to suggest the sort of information which would strengthen or weaken your prediction, and where this may be found; eg 'On the basis of Ms J's account, the previous neglect of her child occurred within the context of a violent marital relationship with an alcohol-dependent husband. No independent description of that period was available at the time of this assessment. Should the social worker's contemporaneous account, or other reliable source, suggest a significantly less disturbed domestic environment than that portrayed by Ms J, then in my view she should be viewed as representing a greater degree of risk than that suggested here.'

Missing material has already been mentioned in the context of other professionals' opinions being unsuccessfully sought. It also becomes important where whole areas of relevant information are systematically unavailable to assessing professionals. It is known that institutional behaviour is not the most reliable predictor of conduct in the community, for example, but some assessors (nursing and prison staff, for example) are routinely expected to extrapolate from that sort of data alone. Armed with research which identifies the best predictors, professionals in this position may well find it useful to lobby their managers and policy-makers for access to more relevant information.

Where the available data restricts the predictive accuracy of an assessment, make this clear, and describe the conditions to which findings do apply; eg 'I have only had access to Mr B's own account of the offences, which portrays him as urinating in a public place while drunk. If this is indeed the behaviour which led to his convictions for Indecent Exposure, then the cost to the public of his reoffending will be fairly low. If the depositions relating to the offence record more deviant, apparently sexually-motivated behaviour while intoxicated, however, the cost to others could be significantly greater: in either case, the probability of re-offending remains high because of his continued alcohol abuse'.

7. Above all, let the evidence drive the conclusion

No doubt everyone reaching a conclusion thinks they have done this. Inevitably, a good proportion will in fact have allowed the 'obvious' conclusion to influence the evidence presented.

When an expert witness (an outside specialist) is brought in to carry out a risk assessment prior to a court hearing, they will be expected to amass all the available information, generate more of their own, test out a number of hypotheses to see which best fits the facts, and as a consequence of all this, reach their conclusions. It is often a lot trickier than it sounds, of course, but it is still like falling off a log in comparison to attempting the same procedure from *within* the case. The outsider is far less likely to hold a position on the desirability of one outcome over another; they are not already frustrated or inspired by months or years of effort, they have little emotional response to those involved, and, perhaps most importantly, if the outcome for case workers is 'Try again', they aren't going to have to do the work!

For those already enmeshed in the case, however, the focus is often narrower (eg 'Has he overcome the denial problem or hasn't he?') and the issues tend to have emotional as well as intellectual weight. Caseworkers might perceive themselves to be associated in some way with the continued failure of the client, may be aware of the drain on their own morale, and might feel with increasing certainty that they have reached the end of the road in terms of motivation (their own and/or the client's). Often, by the time a complex case has reached court, those aiming for opposing outcomes have quite naturally come to see each other as adversaries, and the judgement as representing victory for one side at the expense of the other. Further collaborative work with the client seems impossible to imagine and pointless to attempt. In the opposite type of situation, so much effort has already been expended by both professional and client, that it seems inconceivable to give up, so close to success.

In entrenched and extreme circumstances like these, it is debatable whether the conclusion reached by the involved professionals can ever be the result of rationally weighed evidence; or, indeed, whether it should be. Many caseworkers and clinicians deplore the practice of making the same person responsible both for providing the input and evaluating its effectiveness: they suggest that the roles of client's instructor, therapist, advocate, assessor and judge are incompatible. Should the case reach court, some of those roles are separated out and become clearer, (for example, the counsel for the client taking the advocate's position), but by this time, the feelings of those most familiar with the case are likely to have hardened into concrete positions.

One useful strategy has been to bring in a specialist risk assessor from another agency, often late in the process. This usually has the desired effect of providing a fairly objective view, but a less helpful side-effect can be the undermining of the agency which has been involved from the start and is then responsible for putting into action the recommendations. There is a powerful argument, it seems, for instituting mini-assessments (of risk among other things), by semi-independent individuals or peer review *throughout* the management of a difficult case. A number of organisations already use this procedure, some contracting in a number of sessions from a professional from another employer or discipline, who thus remains independent while developing a clear understanding of the contracting agency's perspective. This can avoid many sources of error and often injects objectivity and creative energy early enough to prevent premature conclusions forming.

CHAPTER NOTES

The *Recommended Further Reading* section at the end of this book contains a selection of key references to the issues covered throughout. The titles of some give clear indications of their content; others are less obvious. For the reader interested in following up particular points, therefore, the following notes link some of the main issues in each chapter with a few of the references which address those issues in more depth.

Chapter 1 The business of risk
John Monahan's (1981) book *Predicting Violent Behaviour: An Assessment of Clinical Techniques* is essential reading on the general principles of risk assessment, and with his later writing elaborates on most areas. Litwack and Schlesinger (1987) develop the major themes and argue some of his more pessimistic views about professionals' accuracy. Campbell (1995) includes a number of references to ethical issues in assessing cases of domestic violence and sexual offending.

Chapter 2 Sources of error
General reading on error in professional decision-making includes Dowey and Elstein (1988). Evans' (1989) book looks further into the cognitive mechanisms involved in the problem-solving process. Klassen and O'Connor (1987) and Lidz et al (1993) describe how self-report improves prediction. Haddad and Benbow (1993) and Monahan (1981) emphasise the need for multi-professional assessments. Glaser (1987) considers a range of methodological issues affecting accuracy, including actuarial v individual indicators. He also highlights the limitations of clinically-derived predictions, as do Cocozza (1978), Lidz et al (1993), Motuik et al (1990) and Blackburn (1984).

Chapter 3 Definition of the target behaviour

Monahan (1981, 1994) and Prins (1991) are among those who emphasise the importance of focusing on the behaviour rather than the individual in prediction. Steadman (1982) and Felson and Steadman (1983) consider situational factors in more depth, as do Salter (1988) and Campbell (1995) in relation to sexual offenders against children and Campbell with those violent to their partners.

Chapter 4 Considering past behaviour

Most published work on risk emphasises the predictive value of past acts. Among those considering specific types of behaviour, Fisher and Thornton (1993) and Barbaree and Marshall (1988) consider child sexual abuse, Sugarman et al (1994) indecent exposure, Litwack and Schlesinger (1987) and Klassen and O'Connor (1988) violent assault, Hawton and Catalan (1987) suicide, Morgan (1979) and Valente (1991) self-injury. Rice and Harris (1992) report that knowledge of the criminal, rather than psychiatric, history appears to be more predictive of future offending in the mentally ill.

Chapter 5 Motivational drive

For the non-psychologist, almost all introductory psychology textbooks provide information on the forces which drive and shape behaviour; key terms will include *functional analysis*, *conditioning*, and *Social Learning Theory*. Monahan (1988) emphasises the need for the prediction of harmful behaviour to be based on accurate formulation.

Motivational theories exist about most categories of harmful behaviour and a literature search will provide details of the most up-to-date range available. Hollin (1989) is a useful general source. Some key works on major offence types include: Finkelhor et al (1984) and Knight et al (1989) on child sexual abuse; Matthews et al (1991) on female sexual abusers; Hingsburger et al (1991) on sexual offenders with learning difficulties; Browne, Davies and Stratton (1988) and Frude (1991) on child physical abuse; Jackson et al (1987) on arson; Petty and Dawson (1989) on sexual aggression; Soothill et al (1976), Rice et al (1990), Prentky et al (1991) and Perkins (1991) on rape; Howells and Hollin (1989) and Monahan and Steadman (1994) on violence, d'Orban (1979) and Bluglass (1990) on infanticide, Levy (1990) on suicide, Marzuk et al (1992) on murder-suicide, Holmes (1989) on serial murder. Heidensohn (1985) is possibly the most eminent amongst those authors who specifically address crimes committed by women.

Chapter 6 Controls and disinhibitors
Finkelhor (1984) was among the first to consider the importance of overcoming internal and external controls in order to commit sexual abuse of children; Murphy (1990) examines the role of cognitive distortions in more depth. J W Swanson (1994) reviews the links between substance abuse and violence, while arguments for and against a causal relationship are also examined in Gelles and Loseke (1993). Seto and Barbaree (1995) discuss the role of alcohol in sexual assault.

Chapter 7 Insights into past offending
Laws' (1989) and Pithers' (1990) work on *Relapse Prevention* are essential reading on understanding and intervening in the offence cycle; these are written specifically in relation to child sexual abuse and sexual assault respectively. The Relapse Prevention model itself, however, originated in the substance abuse field (eg Marlatt 1985) and can be applied to any habitual behaviour. Swanson and Garwick (1990) and Monat-Heller (1992) consider the modifications to this approach when used with sexual offenders with learning difficulties. Novaco's extensive work (eg 1986 and 1994) is central to understanding of the anger process in interpersonal violence and the self-awareness necessary for learning self-control. Improving motivation is explored in Miller and Heather (1986), again through work with substance dependency but widely applicable.

Chapter 8 Cost of the behaviour
A vast amount of literature exists on the short- and long-term effects on the victim of harmful behaviour, but in general this tends to be descriptive rather than quantitative. Published accounts of risk assessment procedures (proposed or already in operation) are more likely to classify *degrees of harm* than are theoretical writings; Iwata et al (1990) on self-harm is an example of the former, while Frude (1991) in chapter 12 is a rare specimen of the latter. Wyatt and Mickey (1988) consider the effect of family support or its absence on those who are sexually abused. Browne and Finkelhor (1986) are among the minority who link the *style* of the offending behaviour with the harm caused. Monahan (1981) and Kemshall and Pritchard (1996) give attention to some of the wider issues of cost to those other than the victim.

Chapter 9 Social and emotional environment

Most of the literature addresses environmental influence in its different forms. Those authors who focus more explicitly on it include Rook (1984); Felson and Steadman (1983) and Monahan (1981 etc) with reference to violence, Finkelhor (1980 etc), Mrazek (1987), Salter (1988) and Fisher and Howells (1993) on child sexual abuse, Telch and Lindquist (1984) and Angela Browne (1987) on domestic violence, Kevin Browne et al (1988) and Frude (1991) on child physical abuse. Smart (1976), Heidensohn (1985), Browne (1987) and Shaw (1992) are among those who consider social factors in women's offending separately.

Chapter 10 Victim factors

It may be argued that sophisticated analysis of victim influence arrived largely through developments in the domestic violence field. Telch and Lindquist (1984) and Browne (1987) are among those authors who consider interpersonal issues in violent relationships. Haller and Deluty (1988) and Wykes (1994) in their work on violence towards professionals also examine triggers by the potential victim of assault, as do Davies and Frude (1993) in their excellent handbook on dealing with face to face assault in the workplace.

Chapter 11 Reliability of detection

The pioneering work by Birchwood (1989 etc) on Early Warning Signs in preventing relapse of mental illness, combined with Pithers' (1990) and Laws' (1989) Relapse Prevention approach to sexual offending, provide some of the central principles and guidelines for practice in this area. Browne et al (1988) and Frude (1991) propose equivalent strategies in cases of child physical abuse; Salter (1988), Mrazek (1987) and Kemshall and Pritchard (1996) in sexual abuse; Howells and Hollin (1989) in managing violence. Cohen et al (1986) and Andrews (1989, 1990) consider factors which predict successful supervision of mentally disordered and other offenders in the community.

REFERENCES
AND FURTHER READING

ANDREWS, D.A. (1982) *The Level of Supervision Inventory (LSI)*. *Report on the Assessment and Evaluation Project*. Toronto: Ontario Ministry of Correctional Services

ANDREWS, D.A. (1989) *Recidivism is Predictable and Can Be Influenced: Using Risk Assessments To Reduce Recidivism*. Forum on Corrections Research

ANDREWS, D.A., BONTA, J. AND HOGE, R.D. (1990) 'Classification for Effective Rehabilitation: Rediscovering Psychology'. *Criminal Justice and Behaviour*, 17:1, 19-52

BARBAREE, H.E. AND MARSHALL, W.L. (1988) 'Deviant Sexual Arousal, Offense History, and Demographic Variables as Predictors of Reoffense among Child Molesters'. *Behavioural Sciences and the Law*, 6:2, 267-80

BARON, R.S., BURGESS, M.L. AND KAO, C.F. (1991) 'Detecting and Labelling Prejudice: Do Female Perpetrators Go Undetected?'. *Personality and Social Psychology Bulletin*, 17:2, 115-123

BIRCHWOOD, M. (1992) 'Early Intervention in Schizophrenia: Theoretical Background and Clinical Strategies'. *British Journal of Clinical Psychology*, 31, 257-278.

BIRCHWOOD, M., SMITH, J. MACMILLAN, F. HOGG, B. PRASAD, R. HARVEY, C. BERING, S. (1989) 'Predicting Relapse in Schizophrenia: The Development and Implementation of an Early Signs Monitoring System Using Patients and Families as Observers, a Preliminary Investigation'. *Psychological Medicine*, 19, 649-656

BIRCHWOOD, M. AND TARRIER, N. (1992) *Innovations in the Psychological Management of Schizophrenia*. Chichester: John Wiley and Sons.

BLACKBURN, R. (1984) 'The Person and Dangerousness' in D.J. Miller, D.E. Blackman and A.J. Chapman (Eds.) *Psychology and Law*. Chichester: Wiley

BLACKBURN, R. (1987) 'Cognitive-Behavioural Approaches to Understanding and Treating Aggression' in K. Howells and C. Hollin (Eds.) (1989) *Clinical Approaches to Violence*. Chichester: John Wiley and Sons

BRENT, D.A. et al (1988) 'Risk Factors for Adolescent Suicide'. *Arch Gen Psychiatry*, 45, 581-588

BROWNE, A. AND FINKELHOR, D. (1986) 'Impact of Child Sexual Abuse: A Review of the Research' *Psychological Bulletin,* 99, 66-77

BROWNE, A. (1987) *When Battered Women Kill*. New York: The Free Press

BROWNE, K., DAVIES, C. AND STRATTON, P., (Eds) (1988) *Early Prediction and Prevention of Child Abuse*. Chichester: Wiley

CAMPBELL, J.C. (Ed) (1995) *Assessing Dangerousness: Violence by Sexual Offenders, Batterers, and Child Abusers*. California: Sage

CARSON, D. (1994) 'Dangerous People: Through a Broader Concept of "Risk" and "Danger" to Better Decisions'. *Expert Evidence,* 3:2, 51-59

CLARK, N.K. AND STEPHENSON, G.M. (1994) 'Rights and Risks: The Application of Forensic Psychology'. *DCLP Issues in Criminological and Legal Psychology,* 33, 3

CLEMENTS, K. AND TURPIN, G. (1992) 'Vulnerability Models and Schizophrenia: the Assessment and Prediction of Relapse' in M. Birchwood and N. Tarrier (Eds.) *Innovations in the Psychological Management of Schizophrenia*. London: John Wiley and Sons

COCOZZA, J.J. (1978) 'Prediction in Psychiatry: An Example of Misplaced Confidence in Experts'. *Social Problems*, 25, 265-76

COHEN, M. et al (1986) *A Base Expectancy Model for Forensic Release Decisions*. Alexandria: Research Management Associates, Inc.

CRIGHTON, J.H.M. (Ed.) (1995) *Psychiatric Patient Violence: Risk and Response*. London: Duckworth

DAVIES, W. AND FRUDE, N. (1993) *Preventing Face to Face Violence*. Leicester: Association for Psychological Therapies

D'ORBAN, P.J. (1979) 'Women Who Kill Their Children'. *British Journal of Psychiatry*, 134, 560-71

DOWEY, J.A. and ELSTEIN, A.S. (Eds.) (1989) *Professional Judgement: A Reader in Clinical Decision-Making*. Cambridge University Press

EVANS, J.St.B.T. (1989) *Bias in Human Reasoning: Causes and Consequences*. Hove and London: Lawrence Gilbaum Associates

EVANS, J.St.B.T. (1989) 'Some Causes of Bias in Expert Opinion'. *The Psychologist*, March

FAVAZZA, A.R. (1989) 'Why Patients Mutilate Themselves'. *Hospital and Community Psychiatry*, 40:2, 137-145

FELSON, R.B. AND STEADMAN, H.J. (1983) 'Situational Factors in Disputes Leading to Criminal Violence', *Criminology*, 21, 59-74

FINKELHOR, D (1984) *Child Sexual Abuse: New Theory and Research.* New York: The Free Press

FINKELHOR, D et al (1986) *A Sourcebook on Child Sexual Abuse.* London: Sage

FISCHOFF, B. et al (1981) *Acceptable Risk.* Cambridge University Press

FISHER, D. AND HOWELLS, K. (1993) 'Social Relationships in Sexual Offenders'. *Sexual and Marital Therapy,* 8, 123-36

FISHER, D. AND THORNTON, D. (1993) 'Assessing Risk of Re-Offending in Sexual Offenders'. *Journal of Mental Health*, 2, 105-17

FRUDE, N. (1988) 'The Physical Abuse of Children'. *Issues in Criminological and Legal Psychology*, 12, 34-44

FRUDE, N. (1991) *Understanding Family Problems.* Chichester: John Wiley and Sons

GARDINER, M., KELLY, R. AND WILKINSON, D. (1996) 'Group for Male Sex Offenders with Learning Difficulties', *NAPSAC Bulletin*, March

GELLER, J.L., FISHER, W.H. AND BERTSCH, G. (1992) 'Who Repeats? A Follow Up Study of State Hospital Patients' Fire Setting Behaviour', *Psychiatric Quarterly*, 63:2, 143-157

GELLES, R.J. AND LOSEKE, D.R. (1993) *Current Controversies on Family Violence.* Newbury Park: Sage Publications

GLASER, D. (1987) 'Classification for Risk' in D.M. Gottfredson and M. Tonry (Eds.) *Prediction and Classification: Criminal Justice Decision Making.* Chicago: University of Chicago Press

GOTTFREDSON, D.M. (1987) 'Prediction' in D.M. Gottfredson and M. Tonry (Eds.) *Prediction and Classification*

GUDJONSSON, G. (1980) 'Psychologist and Psychiatric Aspects of Shoplifting', *Med Sci Law*, 30:1, 45-51

GUNN, J. (1993) 'Dangerousness' in J. Gunn and P.J. Taylor (Eds.) *Forensic Psychiatry: Clinical, Legal and Ethical Issues.* Oxford: Butterworth-Heinemann

HADDAD, P.M. AND BENBOW, S.M. (1993) 'Sexual Problems Associated with Dementia'. *International Journal of Geriatric Psychiatry,* 8, 547-51

HALL, G.C.N. (1988) 'Criminal Behaviour as a Function of Clinical and Actuarial Variables in a Sexual Offender Population'. *Journal of Consulting and Clinical Psychology*, 56, 773-775

HALL, G.C.N. (1990) 'Prediction of Sexual Aggression'. *Clinical Psychology Review*, 10, 229-245

HALLER, R.M. AND DELUTY, R.H. (1988) 'Assaults on Staff by Psychiatric Inpatients: A Critical Review'. *British Journal of Psychiatry*, 152, 174-179

HART, S.D., HARE, R.D. AND FORTH, A.E. (1994) 'Psychopathy as a Risk Marker for Violence: Development and Validation of a Screening Version of the Revised Psychopathy Checklist' in J. Monahan and H. Steadman (Eds.) *Violence and Mental Disorder*. Chicago: University of Chicago Press

HAWTON, K. AND CATALAN, J. (1987) *Attempted Suicide: A Practical Guide to Its Nature and Management*. Oxford: Oxford University Press

HEIDENSOHN, F. (1985) *Women and Crime*. London: Macmillan

HINGSBURGER, D., GRIFFITHS, D. AND QUINSE, V. (1991) 'Detecting Counterfeit Deviance: Differentiating Sexual Deviance from Sexual Inappropriateness'. *The Habilitative Mental Healthcare Newsletter*, 10, 74-79

HOLLIN, C. (1989) *Psychology and Crime: An Introduction to Criminological Psychology*. London: Routledge

HOLMES, R.M. (1989) *Profiling Violent Crimes: An Investigative Tool*. Newbury Park: Sage Publications

HORE, B. (1990) 'Alcohol and Crime' in R. Bluglass AND P. Bowden (Eds.) *Principles in Forensic Psychiatry*. New York: Churchill Livingstone

HOWELLS, K. AND HOLLIN, C. (1989) *Clinical Approaches to Violence*. Chichester: John Wiley and Sons '

HOWITT, D. (1990) 'Risky Sexual Abuse Diagnosis'. *The Psychologist*, January

IWATA, B.A. et al (1990) 'The Self-Injury Trauma (SIT) Scale: A Method for Quantifying Surface Tissue Damage Caused by Self Injurious Behaviour'. *Journal of Applied Behaviour Analysis*, 23, 99-110

JACKSON, H.F., GLASS, C. AND HOPE, S. (1987) 'A Functional Analysis of Recidivistic Arson'. *British Journal of Clinical Psychology*, 26, 175-185

KEMSHALL, H. AND PRITCHARD, J. (1996) *Good Practice in Risk Assessment and Risk Management*. London: Jessica Kingsley Publishers

KLASSEN, D. AND O'CONNOR, W. (1987) 'Predicting Violence in Mental Patients: Cross-Validation of an Actuarial Scale'. Paper presented at the Annual Meeting of the American Public Health Association.

KLASSEN, D. AND O'CONNOR, W. (1988) 'A Prospective Study of Predictors of Violence in Adult Male Mental Health Admissions'. *Law and Human Behaviour* 12:2, 143-59

KNIGHT, R.A., CARTER, D.L. AND PRENTKY, R.A. 'A System for the Classification of Child Molesters: Rehability and Application'. *Journal of Interpersonal Violence*, 44:1, 3-23

KREITMAN, N. AND FOSTER, J. (1991) 'The Construction and Selection of Predictive Scales, With Special Reference to Parasuicide'. *British Journal of Psychiatry*, 159, 185-192

LAWS, D.R. (1989) (Ed) *Relapse Prevention with Sex Offenders*. New York: Guildford Press

LEVEY, S. (1990) 'Suicide' in R. Bluglass and P. Bowden (Eds.) *Principles and Practice of Forensic Psychiatry*. New York: Churchill Livingstone

LIBERTON, M., SILVERMAN, M. AND Blount, W.R. (1992) 'Predicting Probation Success for the First-Time Offender'. *International Journal of Offender Therapy and Comparative Criminology*, 36:4, 335-47

LIDZ, C.W., MULVEY, E.P. AND GARDNER, W. (1993) 'The Accuracy of Predictions of Violence to Others'. *Journal of the American Medical Association*, 269, 1007-11

LITWACK, T.R. AND SCHLESINGER, L.B. (1987) 'Assessing and Predicting Violence: Research, Law and Applications' in I. Weiner and A. Hess (Eds.) *Handbook of Forensic Psychology*. New York: Wiley-Interscience

McMURRAN, M. (1993) 'Alcohol and Crime: The Role of Outcome Expectancies'. Paper presented to the SHSA/SHPAG Clinical Psychology and Offenders Conference

MARLATT, G.A. AND GORDON, J.R. (1985) *Relapse Prevention*. New York: Guildford Press

MARSHALL, W.L., LAWS, D.R. AND BARBAREE, H.E. (Eds.) (1990) *Handbook of Sexual Assault*. New York: Plenum Press

MARSHALL, W.L. et al (1991) 'Treatment Outcome with Sex Offenders'. *Clinical Psychology Review*, 11, 465-485

MARZUK, P.M., TARDIFF, K. AND HIRSCH, C.S. (1992) 'The Epidemiology of Murder-Suicide', *JAMA*, 27:23, 3179-3183

MATTHEWS, J.K., MATTHEWS, R. AND SPELTZ, K. (1991) 'Female Sexual Offenders: A Typology' in M.Q. Patton (Ed.) (1991) *Family Sexual Abuse: Frontline Research and Evaluation*. London: Sage Publications

MELICK, M.E., STEADMAN, H.J. AND COCOZZA, J. (1979) 'The Medicalisation of Criminal Behaviour among Mental Patients'. *Journal of Health and Social Behaviour*, 20, 228-237

MILLER, W.R. AND HEATHER, N. (Eds.) (1986) *Testing Addictive Behaviours: Processes of Change*. New York: Plenum Press

MONAHAN, J. (1981) *Predicting Violent Behaviour: An Assessment of Clinical Techniques.* Beverly Hills: Sage

MONAHAN, J. AND STEADMAN, H.J. Eds (1994) Violence and *Mental Disorder.* Chicago and London: The University of Chicago Press

MONAHAN, J. (1988) 'Risk Assessment of Violence among the Mentally Disordered: Generating Useful Knowledge'. *International Journal of Law and Psychiatry,* 11, 249-5

MONAT-HELLER, R.K. (1992) *Understanding and Expressing Sexuality: Responsible Choices for Individuals with Developmental Disabilities.* Maryland: Paul H Brookes Publishing Co.

MORGAN, H.G. (1979) *Death Wishes? The Understanding and Management of Deliberate Self Harm.* London: John Wiley and Sons

MOTIUK, L.L., BONTA, J. AND ANDREWS, D.A. (1990) 'Dynamic Predictive Criterion Validity in Offender Management'. Paper presented at the Canadian Psychological Association Annual Convention, Ottawa.

MRAZEK, P.B. (1987) 'The Nature of Incest: A Review of Contributing Factors' in P.B. Mrazek and C.H. Kempe (Eds.) *Sexually Abused Children and Their Families.* Oxford: Pergamon Press

MRAZEK, P.B. AND KEMPE, C.H. (1987) *Sexually Abused Children and Their Families.* Oxford: Pergamon Press

MURPHY, W.D. (1990) 'Cognitive Distortions in Sex Offenders' in W.L. Marshall, D.R. Laws and H.E. Barbaree (Eds.) *Handbook of Sexual Assault.* New York: Plenum Press

National Research Council. (1993) *Understanding and Preventing Violence.* Washington, D.C.: National Academy Press

NOVACO, R.W. (1986) 'Anger as a Clinical and Social Problem' in R.J. Blanchard and D.C. Blanchard (Eds.) *Advances in the Study of Aggression.* New York: Academic Press

NOVACO, R.W. (1994) 'Anger as a Risk Factor for Violence among the Mentally Disordered' in J. Monahan and H.J. Steadman (Eds.) *Violence and Mental Disorder.* Chicago: University of Chicago Press

PERKINS, D. (1991) 'Clinical Work with Sex Offenders in Secure Settings' in C.R. Hollin and K. Howells (Eds.) *Clinical Approaches to Sex Offenders and Their Victims.* Chichester: Wiley

PETTY, G.M. AND DAWSON, B. (1989) 'Sexual Aggression in Normal Men: Incidence, Beliefs, and Personality Characteristics'. *Personality and Individual Differences,* 10, 3:355-362

PITHERS, W.D. (1990) 'Relapse Prevention with Sexual Aggressors' in W.L. Marshall, D.R. Laws and H.E. Barbaree (Eds.) *Handbook of Sexual Assault.* New York: Plenum Press

PRENTKY, R.A. et al (1991) 'Developmental Antecedents of Sexual Aggression'. *Developmental Psychopathology*, 1, 153-69

PRINS, H. (1991) 'Dangerous People or Dangerous Situations? Some Further Thoughts'. *Medicine, Science and The Law*, 31:1, 25-37

QUINSEY, V.L. (1980) 'The Baserate Problem and the Prediction of Dangerousness: A Reappraisal'. *Journal of Psychiatry and Law*, 8, 329-340

RICE, M.E., HARRIS, G.T. AND QUINSEY, V.L. (1990) 'A Follow-Up of Rapists Assessed in a Maximum-Security Psychiatric Facility'. *Journal of Interpersonal Violence*, 5:4, 435-448

RICE, M.E. AND HARRIS, G.T. (1992) 'A Comparison of Criminal Recidivism among Schizophrenic and Nonschizophrenic Offenders'. *International Journal of Law and Psychiatry,* 15, 397-408

ROBERTSON, G. (1990) 'Correlates of Crime among Women Offenders', *Med. Sci. Law*, 30:2, 165-174

ROOK, K.S. (1984) 'The Negative Side of Social Interaction: Impact on Psychological Well-Being'. *Journal of Personality and Social Psychology*, 46, 1097-1108

ROY, A. (1986) *Suicide*. Baltimore: Williams and Williams

SALTER, A.C. (1988) *Treating Child Sex Offenders and Victims.* Newbury Park: Sage Publications

SCOTT, P.D. (1977) 'Assessing Dangerousness in Criminals'. *British Journal of Psychiatry*, 131, 127-42

SCULLY, D. AND MAROLLA, J. (1985) ' "Riding the Bull at Gilley's": Convicted Rapists Describe the Rewards of Rape'. *Social Problems,* 32:3, 251-63

SETO, M.C. AND BARBAREE, H.E. (1995) 'The Role of Alcohol in Sexual Aggression'. *Clinical Psychology Review*, 15:6, 545-565

SHEPPARD, D. (compiler), (1995) *Learning the Lessons: Mental Health Enquiry Reports Published in England and Wales Between 1969-1994 and their Recommendations for Improving Practice.* Zito Trust

SMART, C. (1976) *Women, Crime and Criminology: A Feminist Critique.* London: Routledge Kegan and Paul

SOOTHILL, K.L., JACK, A. AND GIBBENS, T.C.N. (1976) 'Rape: A 22-year Cohort Study'. *Medicine, Science and the Law*, 16:1, 62-69

STEADMAN, H.J. (1982) 'A Situational Approach to Violence'. *International Journal of Law and Psychiatry,* 5, 171-86

STEWART, L.A. (1993) 'Profile of Female Firesetters: Implications for Treatment'. *British Journal of Psychiatry*, 163, 248-256

STUART, R.B. (Ed) (1981) *Violent Behaviour: Social Learning Approaches to Prediction, Management and Treatment.* New York: Brunner/Mazel

SUGARMAN, P. et al (1994) 'Dangerousness in Exhibitionists'. *Journal of Forensic Psychiatry,* 5:2, 287-96

SWAFFER, T. (1993) 'A Motivational Analysis of Adolescent Fire Setters'. *Issues in Criminological and Legal Psychology,* 20, 41-45

SWANSON, C.K. AND GARWICK, G.B. (1990) 'Treatment for Low-Functioning Sex Offenders: Group Therapy and Interagency Co-Ordination', *Mental Retardation,* 28, 155-161

SWANSON, J.W (1994) 'Mental Disorder, Substance Abuse, and Community Violence: An Epidemiological Approach' in J. Monahan and H.J. Steadman (Eds.) *Violence and Mental Disorder: Developments in Risk Assessment.* Chicago and London: The University of Chicago Press

TARLING, R. (1993) *Analysing Offending.* London: HMSO

TELCH, C.F. AND LINDQVIST, C.U. (1984) 'Violent Versus Non-Violent Couples: A Comparison of Patterns'. *Psychotherapy,* 21:2, 242-248

THORNTON, D. AND TRAVERS, R. (1991) 'A Longitudinal Study of the Criminal Behaviour of Convicted Sexual Offenders'. *Proceedings of the Prison Psychologists' Conference.* London: HM Prison Service

VALENTE, S.M. (1991) 'Deliberate Self Injury: Management in a Psychiatric Setting'. *Journal of Psychosocial Nursing,* 29:12, 19-25

WARD, D. (1988) *The Validity of the Reconviction Prediction Score.* Home Office Research Study, No. 94. London: HMSO

WEST (1965) *Murder Followed by Suicide.* London: Heineman

WILLIAMS, L.M. AND FINKELHOR, D. (1990) 'The Characteristics of Incestuous Fathers: A Review of Recent Studies' in W.L. Marshall, D.R. Laws and H.E. Barbaree (Eds.) *Handbook of Sexual Assault.* New York: Plenum Press

WYATT, G.E. AND MICKEY, M.R. (1988) 'The Support by Parents and Others as it Mediates the Effects of Child Sexual Abuse' in G.E. Wyatt and G.J. Powell (Eds.) *Lasting Effects of Child Sexual Abuse.* London: Sage Publications

WYKES, T. (1994) *Violence and Health Care Professionals.* London: Chapman and Hall